Maximizing Impact: Success Strategies for Dynamic Nonprofits

By Michelle Mickle Foster, Ph.D.

Paperback ISBN: 979-8-9875055-0-2
Hardback ISBN: 979-8-9875055-1-9
LCCN: 2023900067

This book is dedicated to my parents, Winston and Muline Mickle, my spiritual father Pastor Emanuel Heyliger, the great people of Ferguson Memorial Baptist Church and the Board and staff members of the Kanawha Institute of Social Research & Action, Inc. (KISRA) who served our community with me.

FOREWARD

Michelle Foster and I share common ground in the place of our birth, Guyana, South America, a land of rich cultural heritage and where the emphasis on educational excellence is grounded in our genes. Our meeting was arranged by Providential Design because of a shared commitment to Servant Leadership.

Dr. Foster's qualifications for writing this book extend well beyond her academic credentials. They are grounded in a spiritual stamina that enables her to transcend any challenges that stand in the way. Her zeal for righteousness and good, work in tandem with her passion for social and economic justice.

While her primary intention for writing this book is to give an account of her brand of Servant Leadership, it serves as a model for building resourceful alliances with corporations, community and religious organizations with a call to share a vision for community service. This book also serves to empower the personal pilgrimage of anyone on the path of impactful Servant Leadership.

RT. Rev. Dr. Emanuel Heyliger
Senior Pastor, Ferguson Memorial Baptist Church
Board Chair, Kanawha Institute for Social Research & Action, Inc. (KISRA)
Dunbar, West Virginia

Table of Contents

Appendices

The Appendices are accessible at
www.maximizingwithmichelle.com/appendices

Chapter 1
My Roots

I am a Black, Appalachian immigrant woman living in Charleston, West Virginia - a West Virginian by choice. My life journey began in Guyana, the land of many waters, the only English-speaking country in South America. Guyana is bordered by the Atlantic Ocean, Brazil, Venezuela and Suriname. Once colonized by the Dutch and the British, the country gained independence in 1966. Officially named the Co-operative Republic of Guyana, it is 83,000 square miles in size and has a population of approximately 795,000. Even though in 2017, 41% of Guyanese lived below the poverty line, I am hopeful that with the 2015 oil discovery, economic conditions will improve.

Guyanese ethnic groups include Indians (approximately 40%), Africans (approximately 29%), Multiracial (approximately 20%), Indigenous (approximately 11%), European and Chinese (approximately 0.5%). These ethnic groups contribute to the delectable, flavorful cuisine that I love. Just thinking about pepper pot, cook-up rice, chow mein, curry and roti, bakes and saltfish, metemgee, coconut buns and black cake makes my mouth water and brings a broad smile to my face. These dishes make me nostalgic especially when they are enjoyed with a cold glass of coconut water and complemented with juicy ripe mangoes, chunks of papaya, guavas and genips.

Guyana has a tropical climate. The four seasons I've come to appreciate in the United States are nonexistent there. There is just sunshine and rain. The temperature ranges between 60- and 95-degrees Fahrenheit. Most homes are not air conditioned, but the cooling breezes in the coastal regions make the warm days tolerable. The higher elevations can get cooler at nights, but never as cold as the winters in West Virginia.

I lived with my paternal grandparents, Webster and Amelia Mickle, on Winkle Road, New Amsterdam, on and off from three to 10 years of age. I was their first grandchild and they spoiled me rotten. They had offered to care for me while my parents attended the University of Guyana. Babysitters and nannies were for the wealthy. Low-wealth families relied on family members for childcare during those days.

I attended St. Theresa's Primary School in New Amsterdam from 6 to 10 years old. The schools in Guyana were patterned after the British system. The classes were Preparatory A and B, followed by Standards 1 through 4. I remember walking to and from school daily along a road that was called Back Dam Road. There was a body of water parallel to Back Dam Road. I even walked home for lunch. My journey took me past homes, pastures with cows, and a few small businesses. There were also vendors along the way selling custard blocks and fluties (a Guyanese frozen treat made with fruit juice). My grandparents would give me a few coins to purchase my treats. The distance from home to school was about one mile. My aunts or grandparents walked with me to school in my early years. My grandparents were very protective of me.

I rarely was allowed to leave our yard to play with friends nearby. Thank goodness I had my brother, Winston, Jr. and cousin, Nona, around. I was fortunate that other cousins came to visit from time to time, also.

In Standard 4, students took the Secondary School Entrance Education Examination also known as the Common Entrance Examination to gain entrance to secondary school. I was able to skip two classes/standards during my primary years and was too young to take the Common Entrance Examination when I made it to Standard 4. I had to remain an extra year in that class until I became 10 years of age, the minimum age that someone can sit for the examination. So, I had more time to study my First Aid in English book. This book is memorable to me because it helped me to understand all aspects of the English language. It was the English language Bible of sorts.

Secondary School in Guyana was equivalent to Junior High and Senior High schools in the United States. I performed well on the Common Entrance Examination and was admitted to Queen's College (QC) in 1977. Only the top performing students were admitted to QC. QC is located in Georgetown, the capital city of Guyana. The plan was for me to move back to live with my parents for secondary school. So, gaining admission to QC was in line with the overall plan.

Life at QC was a potpourri of studies and fun. I was the queen of Sal Out. Sal Out is a game with four players on each team on a small pitch with squares/blocks drawn out on the ground. One team is the defender team, and one is the attacker team. Once an attacker is chosen the "Sal Man", they must run from the starting circle to the last square/block without being tagged. If they make it back to the starting circle without being tagged, the rest of their team also become "Sal Men" and get points. We played in the lower level of the main school building.

Along with fun school games, I also participated in track and field sports including the long jump, high jump, discus, shot put and running. I was a member of D'Urban House, which is a group of students that went through the college together and fostered school spirit and group solidarity. Our color was a chocolate brown. Everyone, regardless of their abilities, was encouraged to represent their House during track and field season. Fun times!

Forms 1 through Form 5 were the standard secondary school classes at Guyanese secondary schools. Students entered Form 1 at the beginning of the school year after they completed the Common Entrance exam. QC had exceptional teachers. I still remember the words to French plays that we memorized in Ms. Rollins' class. The quote, "Power corrupts, and absolute power corrupts absolutely" from history class is vivid in my memory. Mid-way through secondary school we had to select a specialty track. I selected the science track because I usually excelled in mathematics and science subjects.

While in Fifth Form, I successfully completed four subjects of the Ordinary Level General Certificate of Education examination and three subjects of the Caribbean Examination Council examination. Generally, students can leave secondary school at

4

this stage. There was no official graduation ceremony per se, but it was the first completion stage. I was only 16 years of age at this time. So, I remained at QC and enrolled in Lower Sixth Form to pursue Advanced Level certifications in science. I don't recall having any interest in leaving QC and finding employment nor were my parents pushing the issue.

Around 1982, my aunt Dolly Chesney submitted the necessary paperwork to sponsor my mom and her younger sister so that they could immigrate to America. The immigration sponsorship process ensures that immigrants are cared for when they arrive in the U.S.

According to the U.S. Citizen and Immigration Services, if you filed an immigrant visa petition for your relative, you must be the sponsor. You must also be at least 18 years old and a U.S. citizen or a permanent resident. You must have a domicile in the United States or a territory or possession of the United States. Usually, this requirement means you must actually live in the United States, or a territory or possession, in order to be a sponsor. If you live abroad, you may still be eligible to be a sponsor if you can show that your residence abroad is temporary, and that you still have your domicile in the United States.

At the time this offer of sponsorship was extended to nine of her siblings, but only my mom and her youngest sister Audrey accepted. Aunt Dolly was the third child of my maternal grandparents, Cleophas and Ismay Amsterdam. She immigrated to America in 1971 after being recruited by a US-based hospital in need of nurses. Prior to her immigration she was a nurse at New Amsterdam hospital.

At 17 years old, I immigrated with my mom, Muline, my sister, Melissa, and Audrey my youngest aunt, to Brooklyn, New York, to pursue the American dream. My father, Winston, Sr., and brother, Winston, Jr., joined us from Guyana two years later.

We left Guyana in 1984 when there were food and other shortages resulting from the government's import restrictions. I remember standing in line with jostling crowds for basics like milk, flour, chicken (sometimes just the backs) and cooking oil rationed out in limited quantities. Power outages were common during this period. We called them blackouts. Even though we lived in a newly built home in the capital city, the water supply did not make it to our house. Daily, we had to carry water in buckets from a supply in the yard to the house for use in the bathroom and kitchen. We each had a bucket of water to bathe and used a small container to pour water over our bodies as best as we could to get clean. There were times when we had no toilet paper and used dampened newspapers instead.

In spite of these experiences, I still experienced joy in my childhood. I have fond memories of our dad taking us to buy ice cream some Saturday evenings from Brown Betty. Even after getting a container of ice cream to eat at home, my brother and I would beg him for cones to eat on the ride back home. One day we were so embarrassed when he yelled, "I cannot buy any cones!" on the sidewalk in front of everyone. I guess he was just tired of our nagging.

After being sponsored by my aunt Dolly, we lived with another aunt, Norma in cramped quarters in her basement until my parents saved up to buy a home. Those early days in Brooklyn were marked with food pantry visits and generic food brands from local grocery stores, but we were happy. We were in America. We discovered that free government cheese, when seasoned right, made the best macaroni and cheese.

We arrived in Brooklyn in April 1984. As we settled there, I had to figure out what to do with my future. My mom, aunts and I decided that I should look for employment until I could enroll in college. I struggled to find employment. I had no marketable skills. I couldn't use a typewriter or take shorthand. I had no work experience, but I was smart and a quick learner. On one of my job search outings with Aunt Norma at Union 1199, when asked what kind of work I was in search of, my response was, "anything." This answer resulted in my family making fun of me for decades afterward. My dad even remembered this response during his remarks at my 50th birthday party. He was proud that I went from not knowing what I wanted to do, to being a President and CEO.

After many job search attempts and without help from any family member, I landed a job at the Burger King Restaurant near the World Trade Center in lower Manhattan in late 1984. I remember feeling very proud when I obtained a perfect score on the mathematics test. I was excited to have my first job even though I was working for minimum wage - $3.35 per hour. I was happy as a lark working on the chicken sandwich station. I used my entire first check to purchase a new wool coat as I disliked the puffy one my mom had bought for me. Working in the fast-food industry was just temporary for me. I knew that I had a good head on my shoulders and that some career was out there for me.

Since I did well in mathematics and science in high school at the prestigious Queen's College in Guyana, I was drawn to study liberal arts and science at New York City Technical College as I had no idea what career I wanted to pursue. I enrolled there in January 1985. I later discovered chemical engineering when a friend suggested it as a good option for my major during a study session, and I transferred to City College of New York (CCNY). Both institutions were a part of the City University of New York (CUNY) system. Before choosing CUNY, my Guyanese high school friend, Kim, tried to convince me to apply to Barnard College and live on campus, where she was, but I was so new to the country that I found commuting to classes from Brooklyn more ap-pealing. I enjoyed college. I could eat my mom's delicious cooking and see my family daily while getting acclimated to my new American life.

I always worked during my undergraduate years. In addition to Burger King, I had stints at Alexander's, a department store at Kings Plaza Mall in Brooklyn, and The Gap in upper Manhattan. I also worked at a childcare center in East New York for a few summers and I was a Work Study student on campus at CCNY.

In the summer of 1989, I worked as an engineering intern at E. I. Dupont Chemical in Delaware. The company had arranged for housing at a generous person's home, and a work colleague transported me to and from work. I took the Amtrak to New York periodically to visit my family. Dupont is also where I was robbed. Within a couple of weeks of the end of my internship, a janitor stole my purse, which contained my wallet and Sony Walkman. I felt violated. I canceled my bank and credit card accounts and had no access to funds to do my back-to—school shopping. Maybe that was a blessing in disguise. Despite this setback, I pressed forward and completed my internship as planned.

During my last year at CCNY (1989–90), I worked part-time at Allied Signal in Morristown, New Jersey. I worked every Friday, traveling from Brooklyn to New Jersey by train and walking over a mile from the train station to the company site.

I have always been very proactive about searching for employment. During my senior year at CCNY, I went to the career services department to get help with my resume and secure job interviews. I also attended various job fairs, even going as far as Maryland for the National Society of Black Engineers job fair. I interviewed for positions in Ohio, Pennsylvania and New Jersey. Working at Proctor and Gamble was my dream, but I could never convince them to make me a job offer.

I graduated from the City College of New York in May 1990 with a bachelor's degree in one hand and a job offer with British Petroleum (BP) America in another. When I left Brooklyn, New York, for Bedford Heights, Ohio, I thought I would be a chemical engineer for the rest of my life.

I settled in Ohio in my first apartment with my boyfriend, and future husband, Steven, who had moved with me from Brooklyn, much to my parents' chagrin. Establishing my own space was exciting. I used my BP moving allowance to purchase furniture and other furnishings locally and from the Lands' End catalog. I was later in awe when I learned that a White colleague who started with BP around the same time had used his moving allowance to invest in mutual funds. At the time I didn't know what a mutual fund was. In Ohio I made new friends who were also transplants to the area. They included Karen and Alfred Leak. Karen was instrumental in connecting me to church, even though I was more of a CME Christian, attending on special days like Christmas, Mother's Day and Easter. But Karen never wavered. She regularly invited me to church and Bible study.

After I had worked for about two years at BP, the company started restructuring. They offered lucrative severance packages and outplacement support to reduce the workforce. I accepted a package and started looking for a new engineering position. I landed one in the Polymer Process Design department at Union Carbide in South Charleston, West Virginia.

When moving from Ohio to West Virginia, my friend Karen encouraged me to find a church home. Little did I know that finding my church home would lead to me discovering my passion.

Chapter 2
Think Long and Hard Before Jumping in: It's a Marathon

All labor that uplifts humanity has dignity and importance and should be undertaken with painstaking excellence.
Dr. Martin Luther King, Jr

This book is about efficiently and effectively operating a community-based nonprofit organization to maximize positive community impact. I spent 18 years running this type of organization in West Virginia, Central Appalachia. The advice I share is from my practical experience on the job and the knowledge I gained during my graduate studies in community economic development and numerous professional development opportunities as a lifelong learner. Appendix A is a detailed checklist on establishing a nonprofit. This book elaborates on the critical steps.

Community-based nonprofit work is not for the weak. It is hard work. It's not a retirement job. To me, it was ministry. Think long and hard before jumping in, or you may not last. A good heart and a willingness to help are not sufficient to bring a nonprofit to fruition. It takes tenacity. You have to be like a tree planted by the river. Though winds and rain and storms may cause you to lean and sway from side to side, you will remain standing, steadfast and immovable when the sun comes out.

Nearly 1 in 5 U.S. businesses fail within the first year, according to the latest data from the U.S. Bureau of Labor Statistics (BLS). With 32.5 million small businesses across the nation, some are undoubtedly bound to fail, whether small or large. Nonprofits are businesses and they must operate as such to increase their likelihood of success. Businesses can be for-profit and nonprofit entities.

A for-profit entity is a business whose primary goal is to earn income and profit for its founders, leaders and employees. The for-profit entity distributes any revenue it makes after paying its expenses and debts to various stakeholders in a predetermined way.

A nonprofit on the other hand is focused on benefitting the community and its residents. Having earned income is rare for a community-based nonprofit, but if and when there is some, it is reinvested in the organization and used to further the mission.

By nonprofit, I mean a 501(c)(3), tax-exempt or charitable organization. According to the Internal Revenue Service, an organization must be organized and operated exclusively for exempt purposes to be tax-exempt under section 501(c)(3) of the Internal Revenue Code. Therefore, none of its earnings may benefit any private shareholder or individual. Nonprofits are separate from the government. They are self-governing and control their own activities. Nonprofits are privately incorporated. There are no owners, and the Board is comprised of volunteers. Nonprofits serve a public purpose and contribute to the public good. They have to refrain from participating in political campaigns of candidates for local, state or federal office and restrict lobbying activities to an insubstantial part of total activities. Additionally, nonprofits cannot operate for the primary purpose of conducting a trade or business that is not related to its exempt purpose.

To operate like a business, a nonprofit may need to get professional help with operations. Community-based nonprofits are usually established to meet pressing community needs, and their staff work tirelessly to pursue their purpose. However, your typical nonprofit will not have internal professional support like a human resources or accounting department. Therefore, retaining external support in these key roles is essential for success.

I highly recommend not trying to do it all alone when you're a new or small nonprofit. Getting the support you need with operations while focusing on your essential services and mission will maximize your impact. Here are some outsourcing options to consider:
- Payroll – Payroll Taxes (941 Filings)
- Property Tax/Business Tax Filings
- Bookkeeping
- Controller/Chief Financial Officer Services
- QuickBooks Support
- Human Resources Support
- Grant Accounting/Reporting

I vividly remember the feeling of relief that I experienced after retaining a Preferred Employer Organization (PEO) to handle our nonprofit's payroll, human resource management, risk management support and benefits administration. We were ramping up for a new program and needed to add over 20 team members. I felt overwhelmed. Working with a PEO helped to dissipate my stress. They helped build our capacity and streamline our operations for a modest fee.

Nonprofits have recordkeeping, filing and disclosure requirements. Recordkeeping includes maintaining financial and non-financial records, especially information on sources of support. Annual filing of an IRS Form 990 is required, except in the case of churches. Unrelated business income tax filings are required if $1,000 or more of gross receipts are from unrelated trade or business. Employment related tax filings are required as with any employer. Nonprofits disclosure requirements include making exemption applications and annual return information available for public inspection. Nonprofits also have to provide written acknowledgments to donors of $250 or more before the donor can claim a charitable deduction. They also have to provide written disclosure to a donor who makes a payment of $75 partly as a contribution and partly for goods and services provided.

"Pros" of 501(c)(3) Designation

There are many great reasons to acquire a 501(c)(3) designation for a nonprofit organization. The best reasons are as follows:
- Exemptions from paying US Federal corporate income tax on donations

- A concurrent exemption from having to pay state income tax
- An exemption from having to pay sales tax on goods and merchandise purchased by the nonprofit
- Assurance to donors that contributions, donations, and gifts are tax-deductible
- Most foundations and grant-making organizations require the designation to qualify for grants
- Some local vendors may also have a policy to make donations or give discounts only to 501(c)3 organizations formally recognized by the IRS
- Non-profit bulk mailing rates, where organizations can save as much as half on mailings
- Since most nonprofit corporations provide for limited liability, Directors and Officers are usually protected from legal actions against the organization
- Having the designation gives your organization credibility

"Cons" of 501(c)(3) Designation

Some cons accompany the 501 (c)(3) designation. A significant amount of paperwork is needed. This includes Articles of Incorporation and corporate bylaws. When the organization is operational, formal meeting minutes must be kept. Setting up and maintaining financial records is also required, along with annual reports required by the Secretary of State and Internal Revenue Service.

Form 1023 is the application for Recognition of Exemption Under Section 501(c)(3) of the Internal Revenue Code. It's expensive to file this application. In 2022 the user fee for Form 1023 was $600 and for Form 1023-EZ (a streamlined application for some organizations) it was $275.

Filing for tax-exempt status takes time and energy. It takes time to prepare the application and the necessary attachments. It then takes the IRS five to seven months to process the application.

If you are considering starting a nonprofit organization, make sure you have the time, energy, tenacity, faith, and wisdom necessary to bring it to fruition and to operate it efficiently and effectively. If you are launching a nonprofit for the glory or because you just want to "help people," your likelihood of success will be slim.

I moved to West Virginia in 1993 after being recruited for a process design engineering position at the Union Carbide Tech Center in South Charleston. Union Carbide Corporation was a chemical and polymers company with more than 2,300 employees in its heyday. The company possessed some of the industry's most advanced process and catalyst technologies and operated some of the most cost-efficient, large-scale production facilities in the world.

Union Carbide primarily produced chemicals and polymers that underwent one or more further conversions by customers before reaching consumers. Some of these materials were high-volume commodities, while others were specialty products meeting the needs of smaller market niches. The end-uses served to include paints and coatings, packaging, wire and cable, household products, personal care, pharmaceuticals, automotive, textiles, agriculture and oil and gas.

The hallmark of Union Carbide's leadership in the chemical industry was a sustained tradition of technological innovation. In 1920 their researchers developed an economical way to make ethylene from natural gas, giving birth to the modern petrochemicals industry. On August 4, 1999, it was announced that Union Carbide would become a subsidiary of The Dow Chemical Company ("TDCC") as part of a transaction valued at $11.6 billion. This transaction closed on February 6, 2001. Since Union Carbide's acquisition by TDCC, Union Carbide has sold most of the products it manufactures to TDCC and is an important part of the Dow family of companies.

As fate would have it, I learned from Elvira Jackson that the pastor of a local church was from Guyana. Elvira was a Carbide employee who came to my office to visit me when she saw my welcome announcement on the bulletin Board in Building 2000 at the Tech Center. One Sunday in the spring of 1993, Steven and I quietly visited Ferguson Memorial Baptist Church (FMBC). Rev. Emanuel Alphonso Heyliger, a fellow Guyanese, was the senior pastor. After accepting God's gift of salvation and joining FMBC in August 1993 during the 75th Church Anniversary celebration, I volunteered to lead various youth programs, starting with Vacation Bible School. I had limited adult experience with organized religion. As a child, my grandmother,

Amelia Mickle, took me to All Saints Anglican Church in New Amsterdam, Berbice in Guyana. So, you could say she planted a seed in me. There was also Sunday School in the afternoons. I attended Sunday School when my brother and I lived with our grandparents in New Amsterdam and when we moved back to Georgetown to live with our parents.

I had some volunteer experience. I was a member of the local chapter of the National Society of Black Engineers. We ran a tutoring program at the Martin Luther King, Jr. Community Center in Charleston. And along with my engineer friend, Marcia Menezes Walker, I ran a teen achievers' program that met on Saturdays at West Virginia State University. So, I was comfortable jumping in where there was a need and helping out without ulterior motives. I had no problems getting used to things.

As I became more engaged in my church volunteer efforts, my other outside volunteer activities diminished. At church, we were engaged in holistic ministry that was grounded in our faith. The more I served, the more my faith in God grew. I am thankful that my faith remained steadfast over the years despite negative, pessimistic people. My excitement about service was shunned by some church members, who often found fault with what I did, perhaps due to their unsuccessful attempts at similar activities. Some even highlighted the fact that I was an outsider. But my enthusiasm never wavered, and Pastor Heyliger provided support, encouragement and guidance. Today I am thankful because my church service led to me finding my purpose. Just know that when God leads you to ministry, he will provide you with whatever you need to make it through any roadblocks on the journey.

In an effort to offer a more structured youth program, I introduced Pioneer Clubs to our church. According to their website, Pioneer Clubs' mission is training children and youth to follow Christ in every aspect of life by providing biblically based and educationally sound resources. Their Christ-centered programs integrate spiritual and personal development to help boys and girls build healthy relationships with caring Christian adults, peers and, most importantly, Christ. We chose Pioneer Clubs for its participative Bible study, Scripture memory, life skills training and emphasis on relational discipleship and outreach. Children of all ages learned about the Bible, enjoyed fun activities, and made new friends. The church was packed with more than one hundred children and volunteers every Tuesday evening for Pioneers. It was an invigorating experience. Michael Jones and Michelle Thompson Brown were co-leaders and friends during this time period. It was through Pioneer Clubs that we discovered literacy challenges among some of the children. This led to a family literacy program and eventually an after-school program.

It got to the point where I couldn't wait for my workday at Union Carbide to end and my volunteer time at the church to begin. Eventually Pastor Heyliger recognized leadership, administration and other gifts in me before I even realized them for myself. He "stirred up my gifts" as the Apostle Paul wrote in II Timothy 1:6.

Pastor Heyliger shared his vision for holistic church ministry and about the church having a nonprofit organization that was established on paper, but not operational. KISRA – Kanawha

Institute for Social Research & Action, Inc., was registered with the State of West Virginia, had articles of incorporation and an IRS tax determination letter. Warren and Cynthia Bush, former church members, who had moved out of state, had set it all up. They had left West Virginia in 1993, the same year I moved to the mountain state. When God gives the vision, he sure does make the provision.

My interest in engineering soon dissipated and I took a leap of faith to full-time service at KISRA, where I developed and implemented programs that strengthened families for almost 18 years. At first, I was living on about half of my engineering salary, but it felt like a light had been turned on in me. I went to sleep at night thinking about KISRA and woke up in the mornings thinking about KISRA. I went from polymer process design to social program design, from chemical engineering to social engineering.

The first program was an after-school program. It was initially run by volunteers a few days per week. After learning about the Community that Cares model, risk factors and protective factors, I was able to secure funding to expand it to a true after-school program, where children were dropped off by the school bus; they then enjoyed a meal, received homework assistance and tutoring and engaged in fun activities. There were field trips, guest speakers, award ceremonies and so much more. Our work with children led to discoveries about the needs of their families. We ultimately expanded our programming to credit and homeownership counseling, workforce development, responsible fatherhood, offender reentry, early childhood

20

development, business development, community housing development, healthcare, mental health care coordination and my favorite project of all time – an urban farm and distribution center. A lot of my time was spent writing grants and securing millions of dollars from federal, state and private sources. A skill I learned on the job since they didn't teach grant writing in engineering school.

We first operated out of the basement of the church and later purchased and transformed a local nightclub into our Kanawha County hub – The Empowerment Center. We developed a HEAL model – Health, Employment, Asset Development and Learning. All of our programs were organized under the HEAL umbrella as we worked to strengthen families in West Virginia, serving as many as 2,500 people per year.

The staff grew from just me working as a contractor for the church, to more than 60, with an annual budget of over $4 million at five locations around the state. My soul was on fire!

Chapter 3

Establish the Needs: Let the Data Guide You

Never start a new program or nonprofit organization to get attention or just a desire to "help people." Instead, create a new program or nonprofit organization to meet specific community needs.

My career path changed when I responded to needs I discovered among children with whom I was volunteering at a church-based program. It was during the operation of the Pioneer Clubs program at Ferguson Memorial Baptist Church in 1996 that I discovered that participants were having difficulty reading. This discovery led to me starting and managing the development of a family literacy program, which led to a full-fledged after-school program, the basis for a multifaceted organization focused on strengthening families in West Virginia. Meeting needs was ministry to me.

A need is a discrepancy or gap between what is and what should be. Unfortunately, there are never enough resources to meet all the needs in a community. However, nonprofits play a vital role in closing some of the gaps. Everyday needs addressed by community-based nonprofits include the following:

- Basic Human Needs – shelters and housing programs for unhoused people; meal programs and food pantries; utility assistance programs

- Health – health and dental care access through community health centers; mental health centers; healthy food access in food deserts through urban farms, farmers markets and local grocery stores; green spaces, playgrounds and exercise facilities; drug prevention and treatment programs
- Education – early childhood education programs; out-of-school time programs; workforce development programs; scholarship and tuition assistance programs; libraries
- Community Economic Development – housing counseling, homebuyer education and housing development; credit counseling; small business loans and technical assistance; community beautification
- Arts and culture – community festivals; visual and performing arts programs

Program planners conduct needs assessments to help identify and select the appropriate intervention to effect a certain level of change. By definition, a needs assessment is a systematic set of procedures used to determine needs, examine their nature and causes and set priorities for future action. Establishing the conditions early in the process makes it easy to build a case for support when you begin your funding search.

Before starting a new program or nonprofit organization, consider conducting a needs assessment to evaluate the potential market for your services:

- Study data from reliable sources to quantify the problem you are attempting to address. Appendix B contain an extensive list of data sources

- Research whether the program you would like to implement is already available in the community you intend to serve and explore collaboration
- Speak to residents about what they see as their community needs
- Speak to existing nonprofits already in the service area as they could be potential referral sources
- Speak with local philanthropic organizations and civic officials about what they see from their vantage point
- Conduct focus groups with people who are likely to benefit from the program/organization

In my early foray into nonprofit work, Helena Lee (West Virginia Division of Criminal Justice Services) introduced me to the Communities that Care (CTC) Model through the local Safe and Drug-Free Communities (SDFC) program. SDFC primarily supported prevention programs and activities. The program provided funding for formula grants to states to support local educational agencies and community-based organizations in developing and implementing programs to prevent drug use and violence among children and youth.

Our community team used this model to conduct a risk and resource assessment, the results of which guided our youth programming and taught us a sound approach to designing community programming. CTC was exactly what we needed. It guided us through a proven five-phase change process. Using prevention science as its base, CTC promotes healthy youth development, improves youth outcomes and reduces problem behaviors. CTC's significant effects on youth health and behavior problems produce long-term economic benefits. For every dollar invested in CTC, $11.14 is returned in the form of lower criminal justice system costs, crime victim costs, health care costs and increased earnings and tax revenues.

CTC helped us to determine how at-risk youth in this area are prone to adolescent problem behaviors mainly substance abuse, delinquency, violence, teen pregnancy and dropping out of school. We identified the following initial risk factors, upon which KISRA's programming was developed: Academic failure, extreme economic deprivation, family conflict and favorable parental attitudes and involvement in the problem behavior.

Collaboration

Collaboration is a key strategy when addressing community needs. One person or one organization cannot do it alone; no man is an island. We are all connected, and we need each other to survive.

Collaboration is about bringing your gifts to the table and sharing them in pursuit of a common goal. It's about bringing all of you, your gifts, your intellect, your passions, your skills, your perspectives, your life experiences, your authentic self, everything about you, to address the challenge and to meet the needs. That is what ministry is all about. For collaboration to work there must be a shared purpose, a shared process and a shared practice.
Collaboration begins with a commitment to work with those who have a shared purpose, defined by both shared values and a shared mission. This is a both/and, not an either/or. Consider

what happens when you collaborate with partners who share your values but not your mission. Initially, you may sense a lot of personal affinities with the group's leadership. Eventually, however, you will experience frustration as your work will constantly move in different directions. Conversely, if you begin to collaborate with partners who share your mission but not your values, you will experience conflict on the level of leadership and process. The ends cannot justify the means when the means embody radically different values. However, when you discover an alignment in both values and mission, you discover a worthwhile prospective partner and should explore collaborative opportunities.

Additionally, collaboration should be defined and designed through a shared process. Once you discover a potential partner with an alignment of values and mission, the next question is, "What are we working on together?" Determine together the goals of your collaboration, detail the resources each group is willing to invest in the work and set expectations for the future.

Effective communication is key to successful collaboration. Determine together how you will communicate, who will be the primary voices in the communication process and ultimately how decisions will be made. As with any healthy relationship, expectations need to be clearly defined and workflow needs to be clearly designed. Defining and designing will ensure that no one dominates the process, while at the same time ensuring that someone is making decisions and the work is moving forward in a way that everyone supports.

Finally, shared practice is needed for a collaboration to work. Shared practice is another way of saying that everyone shows up, makes a meaningful contribution and honors their commitment through the process from beginning to end.

Remember the Pareto's Principle, 80 percent of the work gets done by 20 percent of the people. Shared practice does not mean that everyone invests equally, but it does mean that everyone invests meaningfully.

While at I was at KISRA, we were asked to conduct a community needs assessment of Charleston's West Side on behalf of the Greater Kanawha Valley Foundation. The Foundation retained KISRA for this project to guide the foundation's investment in that particular area of Kanawha County. The assessment was conducted between July and December 2015 and included a review of secondary data, a door-to-door survey of residents and focus group discussions at an elementary school. The Foundation was interested in investing in health, housing and civic engagement initiatives benefiting residents in the following footprint: (1) Hunt Avenue to Grant Street, (2) 3rd Avenue to Bream Street and (3) the Kanawha Boulevard area situated between Hunt Avenue and Bream Street. Therefore, the assessment contained health, housing and civic engagement domains and included the geographic footprint of interest as well as an extended area in the census tract to reach a more representative sample of residents. Demographic and socioeconomic data were also gathered.
Please refer to Appendix C for the complete report on this study.

In 1994, when I raised my hand and volunteered to be the Vacation Bible School director at Ferguson Memorial Baptist Church, I had no idea what a life changing decision I was making. I thought I was just helping because there was a need, but that ministry collaboration was instrumental in me discovering my passion. VBS led to Pioneer Clubs, which led to a literacy program, which led to an afterschool program, which led to numerous programs that strengthened thousands of families through KISRA, which led to me now being at the helm of the Greater Kanawha Valley Foundation where we support programs that reach hundreds of thousands in West Virginia and beyond. Throughout my journey collaboration was key. I am so blessed to have had people like Michelle Thompson Brown, Maxine Brown, Angela Dobson, Michael Jones, Carl Chadband, Verbieann Hardy, LaTausha Taylor, GA McClung, William Lipscomb Sr. and Maria Terrell, just to name a few, to collaborate with in meeting community needs.

Chapter 4
Vision, Mission and Values: Foundational Organizational Elements

After identifying the needs to be addressed, composing a vision, mission, and values are key next steps. These are essential elements of a well-functioning nonprofit organization.

Vision Statement

A vision statement looks forward and creates a mental image of the ideal state the organization wishes to achieve. It is a vivid mental image of what you want your organization to be at some point in the future, based on your goals/desired outcomes and aspiration. It gives shape and direction to the organization's future.

The KISRA vision is a state of West Virginia with productive, engaged and caring families in thriving communities.

Sample Visioning Exercise:
- Write today's date, three years in the future
- Describe the organization in the present tense from that date

- If you were 100% successful, what would that look like?
- Describe it in clear detail, such that if you explain it to another person, they can feel it and see it
  - o Think about funding, processes, systems, management communication and marketing. What are people saying about you?
- What does success look like to you? If you are successful, how would you know?
- What qualitative or quantitative measures will tell you that you have achieved success?

Whenever I think about vision, I think of Habakkuk 2:2 in the Bible which states, "And the LORD answered me, and said, Write the vision, and make *it* plain upon tables." Writing down the vision for your organization is critical. Writing the vision down helps to imprint it on your mind. A written vision will give you the correct directions and coordinates you need to follow to get to your desired destination. It will give you the inspiration and motivation you need to push through life's toughest challenges. A written vision will motivate you to take action; provide a filter for other opportunities; and help you overcome resistance. And when we do write a vision down, it needs to be in plain, simple to understand language that even a fifth grader can grasp it.

Creating a vision that is clear and simple to understand will eliminate confusion that can hinder its progress. A plain vision will energize and ignite excitement in everyone who is connected to it, because the fact that it is being written on the tables/tablets means that it is being shared with others around.

It is like putting a call out for people who want to run a race because they are somehow connected with the vision that is written. They believe in the cause, so they get the right gear (clothing and shoes), they get the right sustenance and go to the starting line. Once there, it's time to run. And not only you, running by yourself, but the vision will be so inspiring that the others who read it will want to run with it, in eager anticipation. It could get lonely running by yourself; that's why having a team to run with is so important.

I have always been a "big girl." Always the largest girl in my class. I am not built like an athlete even though I participated in track and field sports in high school and was encouraged to do so as a part of the "house" system at Queen's College. I competed in shot put, javelin, long jump and high jump.

Nevertheless, I was inspired to complete a Couch to 5K program and ran my first 5K race on June 30, 2012. We were scheduled to run a June 29, 2012, race on Kanawha Boulevard in Charleston, West Virginia, but the Derecho hit. My training group was so disappointed when we couldn't run. But discovered the June 30th race in St. Albans and ran that one instead. I ran several 5K races after that first race and even ran the 5K and 8K races of the Charleston Winter Series, but then I avoided running for about five years. However, as a part of my new weight loss plan, I started running again earlier in 2022. I went back to Genesis Running and trained for a 5K in nine weeks. I continued running and finished my first 10K race after training for another seven weeks.

I used the principles I learned during the 5K training group to continue training for a 10K. Training for and completing a 10K has been a written vision of mine for years and I finally got it done! I felt so accomplished. Completing this milestone reinforced the fact that a vision will speak, even though it may be delayed. Through the first nine weeks of training, my running coach, Matthew Young, drummed in my head the importance of pacing myself in a race. He would always say, "easy start, strong finish." This means that when you are running, you shouldn't start off at a pace that you can't sustain. It's better to start easy, take your time, then build up speed as you go, so that you will endure to the finish line. He also taught us to "run our own race." My race is mine. Your race is yours. I'm not trying to run your race at your pace. I'm doing me! You better do you!

Habakkuk 2:3 reads, "For the vision is yet for an appointed time, but at the end it shall speak, and not lie: though it tarry, wait for it; because it will surely come, it will not tarry." This verse suggests that the race to our vision is not a sprint, but an endurance race. You can't start running for the first time this week and then next week run a marathon. You're not going to last! And you can't start running before you see the vision.

Mission Statement

A mission statement is a concise explanation of the organization's reason for existence. It is an action-oriented statement declaring the purpose an organization serves to its audience and its overall intention.

The best nonprofit mission statement succinctly captures the why, who and how of the organization. It should answer the following questions:
1. Why does the organization exist?
2. Who does it serve?
3. How does it serve them?

The mission supports the vision and serves to communicate the purpose and direction to a wide variety of stakeholders. A mission statement is a roadmap for the organization's vision statement.

There are many reasons why mission statements are important to nonprofits. Here are a few:

1. They clarify purpose and determine direction

A good mission statement serves as a North Star for a nonprofit. It's a foundation for your strategy and a guiding tool for many activities: from recruiting your team to marketing and outreach. By definition, you can't prioritize everything, and your nonprofit mission statement helps you clarify what to focus on. As a non-profit leader, it is often tempting to go after new funding for the latest and greatest offering from a grantmaker. Tread lightly. Think twice before jumping on the bandwagon if the funding is not in line with your mission. Mission creep (a gradual shift in objectives) will detour you from your destiny.

2. They motivate staff, supporters, board and volunteers

Mission statements influence how organizations are perceived by the public and how team members think of their roles. A mission statement influences and shapes your organizational culture. Organizational culture impacts employee happiness which then impacts employee retention. People want to believe in the work that they do. They want to feel valued and included. Their first feeling of belonging can be stimulated by the mission statement. Belonging is a sense of connection one has to a group. Do I feel like I fit in? Am I considered a valued member of the team? Am I accepted for who I am? Belonging and inclusion are related. You can't have belonging without inclusion.

Even though my life journey did not begin in West Virginia, I fit in at work and in my community. I feel like I am a valuable team member and community contributor and accepted for who I am. Hence, I have adopted West Virginia as my home since 1993.

3. They provide a template for decision making

A mission statement is to an organization what a compass is to an explorer. If designed well, it will provide your nonprofit with a framework for making decisions throughout the organization, and to focus your energy and attention. Your mission statement can help you evaluate options and decide what's best for your organization according to your vision for the future. All activities should be in line with your mission. New projects and partnerships should be in line with your mission. Otherwise, step away from the table. You only have so many hours in the day. Use your time on activities to move forward your mission.

4. They send out a powerful message to the public

In one or two sentences, your mission statement sums up the essence of your organization. It speaks volumes about what you stand for and what makes you unique. It should make people want to know more about your organization and support your work, which will enhance your sustainability as you work to meet the needs.

Tips on Writing a Great Mission Statement

1. Make it clear

Your mission statement should be unambiguous, simple and easy to understand. Use simple and concrete language and avoid buzzwords and jargon. Remember the KISS principle — Keep It Simple Stupid.

2. Make it concise

A well-crafted mission statement should be brief and to the point. Shoot for 5-15 words, 20 words max. Avoid words greater than 12 letters or 4 syllables long.

3. Make it informative

A mission statement should, above all, inform others about what you do and guide your team members and stakeholders. It doesn't matter how concise or catchy it is if it doesn't do that.

4. Welcome participation

Include participation from all parts of your organization including your employees, Board of directors, volunteers, long-term supporters and friends of the organization. Consider convening a focus group if your organization is larger.

5. Review it frequently

Revisit your nonprofit mission statement at least annually so you ensure that it still represents your programming.

The mission of KISRA is to strengthen families. We had longer ones in the early years but thought a simple statement capturing the essence of our services was most appropriate.

Values

Values are the organization's beliefs in action. Values guide the behavior of staff and volunteers as they take action to realize the vision and mission.

Core values are the deeply ingrained principles that guide all of an organization's actions; they serve as its cultural cornerstones. Collins and Porras succinctly define core values as being inherent and sacrosanct; they can never be compromised, either for convenience or short-term economic gain. Core values often reflect the values of the organization's founder. They are the source of an organization's distinctiveness and must be maintained at all costs. These were the core values we developed at KISRA:

- spirituality
- commitment to excellence
- faith
- integrity
- respect for all people
- continuous improvement
- collaboration to maximize impact
- transparency
- accountability

Chapter 5
Get the Right People on the Team

In spring 1998 I was terminated from my engineering position at Union Carbide. Yes, terminated. To be honest I had lost interest in engineering, and I guess it showed in my work. My manager told me I had even been observed dozing off during a major group meeting; Must have been after an evening of volunteering at the church. I was written up for the sleeping incident. I was then reassigned to a position that involved frequent travel to the Louisiana plant. During this time, I was also receiving frequent calls for "random" drug testing. Of course, I was never on illegal drugs, my heart was just elsewhere.

I was devasted after being terminated, but I didn't have any desire to look for a new engineering position. People get fired all the time. Life would go on. I still had my health. I still felt the presence of God in my life. My life had purpose. I still had a sound mind. I could have looked for another engineering position anywhere in the country, but I didn't. I had discovered my passion and it was community ministry or social engineering as I called it. The termination was a blessing. All things do work together for good to those who love God and for those who were called according to his purpose. I believe God had a different calling for my life. I decided to take Pastor Heyliger up on his offer to work for Ferguson Memorial Baptist Church. For months, prior to my termination, he would ask me, what would it take for you to come and work for the church?" I would just laugh, thinking he was crazy, the church couldn't afford me. But something had changed.

After the termination I would spend long hours at the church working on various projects living on my severance check. My official title was Church Administrator. This was during the time of the mortgage burning and cornerstone laying ceremonies at the church. I then started building the infrastructure and the early programs for KISRA.

When Pastor Heyliger realized I wasn't going anywhere, he convened the church leadership to see how they could pay me to serve as Church Administrator and Executive Director of KISRA. Pastor Heyliger, Deacon Philip Heyliger (deaconate chair), Deacon Guy Brown (trustee chair) and Melvin Jones (treasurer) met in the pastor's study and committed to a $30,000 annual contract for me. This was a little more than half my engineering salary. They even committed to borrowing the funds if the church wasn't able to sustain me, but they never had to. Samuel Williams, the church janitor at the time, was a skilled builder. He converted the former nursery in the back of the church into my office. I am forever grateful that these men of God believed in my abilities and invested in me to bring to fruition Pastor's vision for holistic ministry. Even though I was earning significantly less, I was ecstatic, and I never missed a meal or a mortgage payment. I was walking by faith, and it felt so good!

I even filed for divorce during this time. My husband, Steven, had taken a job in Washington, DC after unsuccessfully being able to maintain a job in West Virginia. I was the primary bread winner for our entire relationship. I used birth control and was never interested in having children because I felt so burdened with all the responsibilities of the relationship. I tolerated him for years because I had a fear of being alone. But I was through with him. He was living and working away from home, visiting infrequently, and not sending any money home to maintain the household. What was the point? After I saw how God took care of me during my career transition, I had the courage I needed to file for divorce without the use of an attorney. I had come to my senses. Enough was enough.

As I got situated in my new career with KISRA, I soon realized I had to build a team. Angela Dobson, who was serving as the church's Financial Secretary, agreed to join me at KISRA in 2000. Pastor Heyliger was receiving a monthly check for his work with Mission West Virginia. He had it directed to KISRA so that we could afford to pay Angela. Angela had bookkeeping, computer, and administrative skills. She was also hardworking, conscientious and a great thought partner. She was by my side the entire time I was at KISRA.

Social impact is possible when the right people come together and focus like a laser beam on a challenge. Be deliberate and strategic as you assemble your team. Get the right team members in the correct positions for new organizations before solidifying the mission and vision. Leaders of existing organizations should take the time necessary to identify new team members who will fit the organizational culture and complement the existing team.

Your team includes Board members, staff and volunteers. These stakeholders must subscribe to the mission and vision of the organization and commit to its success. In addition, they should have a heart for the people they intend to serve. All team members should have a position description so that everyone can stay in their own lane and promote the smooth operation of the nonprofit.

Board of Directors

I was thankful for a supportive Board of Directors at KISRA. The Board is legally, financially, and morally responsible for the operations and conduct of the nonprofit. The Board is answerable to the government agencies that regulate and monitor nonprofit organization. Given that they have such important roles, Board members should be carefully selected and never randomly identified. A nominating committee should be convened for this purpose. The committee should consider demographics, knowledge, skills, attitudes, talents and geographic location. Having an attorney, accountant, marketing/communications professional and professionals who can assist in achieving the organization's mission is recommended. Typical Board responsibilities include the following:

- Attend board and committee meetings regularly
- Define/redefine philosophy, mission, and policies
- Monitor programs vis-a-vis the mission
- Participate in strategic planning to achieve the mission
- Oversee finances
- Be an informed advocate
- Share time, talent, and influence

- Financially contribute to the organization and encourage others to do likewise
- Review the CEO/Executive Director's performance
- Actively participate in sustainability strategies
- Succession planning

Most importantly, Board members are fiduciary agents. They are legally responsible for the organization and are expected to manage it as, "responsible prudent persons."

The executive director/CEO should conduct orientations for all board members before they start serving. Board members should also receive a board book. At a minimum, the board book should contain the following:

- Bylaws
- Mission, Vision and Values
- Most Recent Audited Financial Statements
- Most Recent IRS Form 990
- Organizational Chart
- Board Member Contact List
- Board Member Position Description
- Board Meeting Schedule
- Most Recent Board Meeting Minutes
- Annual Organizational Budget
- Strategic Plan
- Executive Director/CEO Contact information
- Organization Web Site and Social media Handles

With regards to the size of the Board, it depends on the minimum required by the state and the overall reach of the organization.

An average size is 13 and includes officers – chair, vice-chair, treasurer and secretary – and directors. Most of the work of the Board gets done in committees. Common committees include executive, budget and finance, development and personnel.

Common Nonprofit Board Problems

1. Veering off the mission

The most important guideline for a Board on all decision making is the mission statement. If the mission is not central at every Board meeting, it is easy to lose focus on the true purpose of the organization. I recommend including the organization mission on all board meeting agendas. For example, if you are a youth-serving educational organization you shouldn't accept funds for an adult health project.

2. Complacency

A core obligation of every Board member is participation. Some symptoms of complacency might include Board members who miss meetings, fail to participate in discussions and put off assignments. The board chair should reach out to board members who miss meetings to assess their interest in board service and remind them of their commitment. If nothing changes then the board member should be asked to step down.

3. Misguided motivations

Board members must always put the organization first. Allowing personal preferences to affect decision making places the organization in a secondary role in a Board member's mind. Misguided and unethical motivations, undeclared conflicts of interest, and the pursuit of personal benefit may endanger the organization's tax-exempt status. Conflicts of Interest disclosures should be completed annually. For example, a board member shouldn't push the CEO to hire his marginally qualified relative.

4. Multiple voices

A Board only has authority as a group. Boards speak with one voice, which is formulated through deliberation. Individual Board members are bound by the collective decision. Differing opinions need to be resolved in the Boardroom, not declared outside to constituents, the media or program participants. Only the CEO should speak for the organization and the Board chair should be the primary board contact.

5. Micromanagement

One of the key duties of a Board is to hire a competent chief executive to run daily operations. Part of this duty assumes that there is a valid job description and a performance evaluation process in place. The Board's role is to oversee that the organization is well run; not to interfere in the domain of the chief executive.

Board members should stick to their policy-making roles and let the chief executive manage the organization. All staff report to the chief executive and only the chief executive reports to the board and she should be the primary staff contact for the board.

6. Limitless terms

Every Board must accept and even thrive on change. New perspectives and different ideas keep the Board and organization moving forward. Term limits can help the Board avoid stagnation. Two to three, three-year terms are typical.

7. Lawless governance

Nonprofit tax-exempt organizations must heed federal, state and local regulations, as well as their own bylaws. It is the Board's responsibility to make sure that all laws are respected. The Board needs to assure that the organization files its IRS Form 990 correctly and on time; that employment taxes are withheld regularly; and that official documents are saved appropriately. If the Board fails to oversee adherence to these regulations and the creation of appropriate policies, it may become liable for wrong doings.

Grantmakers check on whether applicants are current on their federal, state and local filings as a part of the grant review process. Not being current can affect your organization's ability to secure funding. For example, grantmakers will not award a grant to your organization if they discover that you have a habit of not paying your employment taxes.

8. No Board self-assessment

By studying its own behavior, sharing impressions, and analyzing the results, the Board is able to lay the groundwork for self-improvement. Failing to assess its own performance, the Board is unable to define its strengths and weaknesses. As a by-product, self-assessment also can enhance the Board's team spirit, its accountability, and its credibility with funders and other constituents.

An assessment can be incorporated into the strategic planning process.

9. Knotted purse strings

Asking for and giving donations are natural aspects of being a Board member in most 501(c)(3) nonprofit organizations. Boards that don't have a 100 percent personal contribution rate, have failed the ultimate commitment test. If the Board is not supporting the organization whole-heartedly, how can it convince others to do so? Board members should be financially contributing to the organization, getting others to financially contribute to the organization or getting off the board if they aren't doing any of the above.

Diversity, Equity and Inclusion

Be sure to consider diversity, equity and inclusion in the process of developing or building your team. Research has shown that diverse teams produce more significant outcomes. Being mindful of diversity, equity and inclusion during the organization building phase will reap great rewards later on your journey.

Diversity is about including people like me. Different people. People who did not attend your high school or university, but people with personal assets and intellectual capital to contribute to your organization.

You are mistaken if you feel diversity is about attacking the white male. Diversity is not about getting "them" into your corporate culture. It's not about assimilation. Diversity is about creating a culture where everyone can thrive, contribute to an organization and serve your ever-more diverse customers. Diversity is about integration and multiculturalism. Diversity is not lowering standards but widening the net and sometimes raising or re-writing them. As the prophet Isaiah wrote, "let us enlarge the tent, lengthen our cords, and strengthen our stakes."

I'll share six nuggets about diversity and inclusion with you.

1. Diversity is a fact

The United States is becoming more racially and ethnically diverse; increase your awareness and plan for it now or be left behind. Diversity is not another fad. If you think it is, good luck with that. Have you seen the demographic projections?

Millennials (ages 23 to 38) started outnumbering Baby Boomers (ages 55 to 73) in 2019. Now in their young adult-hood, Millennials are more educated, more racially and ethni-cally diverse, and slower to marry than previous generations were at the same age. The "post-Millennial" generation is already the most racially and ethnically diverse generation, as a majority of 6- to 21-year-olds (52%) are non-Hispanic whites. Blacks, Asians, Hispanics and other racial minorities will make up most of the population by 2050.

We all must accept the fact that our country is becoming more multicultural. For organizations to remain relevant and compet-itive, they must be open and accepting of different people.

2. Diversity is more than race and gender

Diversity in the workplace is about bringing together people who are different from each other to maximize synergy and impact. I refer to people with unique characteristics, backgrounds, experiences and perspectives. It is beyond just race and gender.

You see, we are all comprised of various dimensions of diversity. Our personality is, at our core, an innately unique aspect that gives each person their style – in my case, my openness, conscientiousness and somewhat introverted ways. Our personality permeates all the outer layers.

Next are our internal dimensions, which are the ones we have little or no control over. They include demographics like race, age, gender, sexual orientation, physical ability and ethnicity. External dimensions are the third layer, made up of external, personal and societal influences; they shape who we are, like education, income, geographic location, work experience, parental status, marital status, recreational habits, physical appearance and religion. Finally, organizational dimensions encompass those characteristics we typically use to define ourselves at work, like the type of work we do, seniority, work location and management status.

I hope you will agree that diversity is more complex than race and gender. These dimensions of diversity lead to the assumptions we make, drive our behaviors, and ultimately impact others. Consequently, the better we understand ourselves and others, the more our interactions and decisions will be effective.

3. Driving for more diversity and inclusion results in equity

Inclusion in the workplace is not just window dressing. Inclusion is not just having a certain number of people of color. Inclusion is not just checking the box. Inclusion is the act of creating environments in which any individual or group can feel welcomed, respected, supported and valued to participate fully. An inclusive and welcoming climate embraces differences and offers respect in words and actions for all people. While an inclusive group is, by definition, diverse, a diverse group isn't always inclusive.

Diversity is. Diversity is the human aspect, and we are all diverse. However, inclusion is the environment, and the atmosphere people experience and in which they work.

Inclusion is the ability of diverse people to raise their perspectives authentically and for those voices to matter and affect decisions within majority-group settings. The organizational culture has to enable that to happen. It is the initiative of majority-group members to access non-majority voices in the latter's settings and through their informational vehicles so that majority-group members enlarge their understanding of issues and relationships. Neither of these approaches ensures the absence of disagreement, but inclusion promises a broader view of the world and a more democratic decision-making process.

Recruiting and hiring top, diverse talent isn't enough; we must create an inclusive work environment where those people feel valued, respected and treated fairly and have equal opportunities to succeed.

Diversity without inclusion will fail to attract and retain diverse talent. Moreover, it doesn't encourage diverse employees to bring their whole selves to work, thereby failing to motivate their participation and do their best work.

Driving for more diversity and inclusion results in equity. Equity is giving people what they need to succeed. Equity is freedom from bias or favoritism. It is fair treatment, access, opportunity and advancement for all people. It is striving to identify and eliminate barriers that have prevented the full participation of some groups. Improving equity involves increasing justice and fairness within the procedures and processes of institutions or systems and their distribution of resources.

Please do not confuse equality with equity even though they both seek the same outcome – fair treatment for everyone. Equality is about everyone getting the same opportunities, access and resources. Equity acknowledges that not everyone needs the same things, because everyone did not begin at the same starting line.

To summarize, diversity is the "who;" equity is the "how"; and inclusion is the "what."

4. Leadership is accountable for diversity and inclusion

Strong leadership is central to achieving diversity and inclusion goals and can affect the overall performance of an organization. Leadership can influence the culture of an organization and the ecosystem in which it operates. Therefore, placing core business leaders and managers at the heart of your diversity and inclusion effort is imperative.

Through fairness and transparency, the leader can ensure a level playing field in advancement and opportunity in pursuit of true meritocracy. The leader can deploy analytical tools to build visibility, thereby ensuring that promotions, pay processes and criteria are transparent and fair. It is the leader who can work to meet diversity targets across long-term workforce plans. It's up to leaders to promote openness and tackle microaggressions. When I say "microaggression," I am referring to commonplace daily verbal, behavioral or environmental slights, whether intentional or unintentional, that communicate hostile, derogatory or negative attitudes toward stigmatized or culturally marginalized groups.

Leaders can tackle microaggressions by upholding a zero-tolerance policy for discriminatory behavior such as bullying and harassment— and actively build the ability of managers and staff to identify and address microaggressions. Leaders can also establish norms for what constitutes open, welcoming behavior. So, all leaders should be held accountable for progress on diversity and inclusion.

5. Diversity improves business performance

The evidence is irrefutable that diversity and inclusion are good for the bottom line and in the case of nonprofits, the triple bottom line.

Research shows that diverse companies are more likely to outperform their peers financially. When it comes to gender diversity, a 2019 analysis finds that companies in the top quartile of gender diversity on executive teams were 25 percent more likely to experience above-average profitability than peer companies in the fourth quartile. The higher the representation of women, the higher the likelihood of outperformance. Companies with more than 30 percent women on their executive teams are significantly more likely to outperform those between 10 and 30 percent women. In turn, these companies are more likely to outperform those with fewer or no women executives.

When it comes to ethnic and cultural diversity, the higher the ethnic and cultural representation, the higher the likelihood of outperformance; companies in the top quartile outperformed those in the fourth quartile by 36 percent in terms of profitability. In addition, there is a higher likelihood of outperformance difference with ethnicity than with gender.

6. Nurturing a sense of belonging and community will improve retention

Belonging is a sense of connection one has to a group. Do I feel like I fit in? Am I considered a valued member of the team? Am I accepted for who I am? Belonging and inclusion are related. You can't have belonging without inclusion.

As I said earlier, my life journey did not begin in West Virginia. However, I've lived here since 1993 because my community and I are a good fit. I feel like I am a valuable team member and community contributor and accepted for who I am.

I implore you to build a culture where all employees feel they can bring their whole selves to work. Managers, communicate and visibly embrace your commitment to multivariate forms of diversity, building a connection with diverse individuals and supporting employee resource groups to foster a sense of community and belonging.

Your diversity strategies and plans are opportunities to differentiate your organization from your competition. Rise to the occasion. Finding and retaining good employees can be challenging these days. However, an organization that values diversity and is inclusive is an organization that is a "good place to work" for everyone.

Diversity in professions/skills is also recommended for nonprofit Boards of directors. Ideally, nonprofit Boards should include people from the following disciplines: law, accounting, marketing, government, clergy, and communications.

Team Effectiveness

An effective team is comprised of people with different skills and different personality types. For example, consider team members who are:

- **Results-oriented.** Team members who naturally organize work and take charge; tend to be socially self-confident, competitive and energetic.
- **Relationship-focused.** Team members who naturally focus on relationships, are attuned to others' feelings, and are good at building cohesion; tend to be warm, diplomatic and approachable.

- **Process and rule followers.** Team members who pay attention to details, processes and rules; tend to be reliable, organized and conscientious.
- **Innovative and disruptive thinkers.** Team members who naturally focus on innovation, anticipate problems and recognize when the team needs to change; tend to be imaginative, curious, and open to new experiences.
- **Pragmatic.** Practical team members, hard-headed challengers of ideas and theories; tend to be prudent, emotionally stable and level-headed.

Position Descriptions

Take the time to prepare position descriptions for all staff and volunteers. A well-written position description not only outlines what is expected of an employee or volunteer, but also helps you define the necessary skills for the position. Developing position descriptions is fundamental to good management practices.

All employees like to know what is expected of them and how they will be evaluated. Creating a position description often results in a thought process that helps determine how critical the position is, how this particular position relates to others and identifies the characteristics needed by an employee filling the role.

A position description typically outlines the necessary skills, training and education needed by an employee. It will spell out duties and responsibilities of the job. Once a position description is prepared, it can serve as a basis for interviewing candidates, orienting a new employee or volunteer and evaluating job performance. Using position descriptions is part of good management.

Refer to Appendix D for a sample position description document.

Chapter 6
Leadership Essentials

To be an effective leader you must be a good listener. Charles Patton, Former Chief Operating Officer, Appalachian Power Company

I am the leader I am today because Pastor Heyliger saw leadership skills within me before I recognized them in myself and gave me opportunities to activate them in.

What is leadership?

Leadership is a dynamic condition that can be developed and demonstrated by any person willing to choose to adopt a certain mindset and implement certain key skills and competencies. Leadership is the process of influencing the activities of an individual or a group in efforts toward achieving a goal in a given situation.

Leadership is a set of skills or traits. It is a function of knowing yourself, having a vision that is well communicated, building trust among colleagues and taking effective action to realize your own leadership potential. It is about articulating visions, embodying values and creating the environment within which things can be accomplished.

Myths about leadership
Myth #1: Leaders work smarter, not harder.

There are ways to work smarter – prioritizing, time management, delegation, etc. However, successful people DO work hard. Nothing great has ever been achieved without working hard. The leader is usually first one in and last one out. Building KISRA was hard work. I was learning, designing, finding funding, implementing and evaluating several programs. I eventually recruited a team to assist, but it was still my responsibility to ensure we were being effective and efficient. Cutting corners and not doing a thorough job were not options. Through their dedication, leaders inspire people around them.

Myth #2: Leaders have all the answers.

The best leaders have a clear understanding of their own limitations. They know that success is a team sport and there is no such thing as a self-made man. They realize that it takes a diverse team to truly innovate.

Myth #3: Great leaders are always in the spotlight.

It is true that if you are a leader of the organization there is an expectation that you will also be a spokesperson. But leadership comes in many forms. You don't have to be on the organization's executive team to be a leader. True leaders (whether they are at the helm or not) are humble. They don't much care about the spotlight. They care about and are focused on the results.

In his book *Good to Great* Jim Collins says that exceptional leaders channel their ego needs away from themselves and into the larger goal of building a great organization. "It's not that

[they] have no ego or self-interest," says Collins. "Indeed, they are incredibly ambitious – but their ambition is first and foremost for the institution, not themselves." These amazing leaders, Collins found, "are a study in duality: modest and willful, humble and fearless."

Myth #4: Leaders are always on.
Even though great leaders work hard, they realize that they need the space to be able to strategize, to think to create. *"Restore connection is not just for devices,"* cautions Arianna Huffington. *"It is for people too. If we cannot disconnect, we cannot lead."* Leaders like Steve Jobs and Bill Gates were known to go away for extended periods of time to reconnect with themselves, their vision and their ideas. Leaders need to find that place of wisdom, strength and real connection (with themselves and others) and they need to lead from that place. Smart leaders also build the culture of creativity through encouraging their employees to take time to reflect. It took me a while to realize that I needed to take time off, but I finally got it. Remember, if you drop dead today, life will go on. Take time for restoration. Take time to smell the roses.

Are leaders born or made?

Leaders are mostly made. Best estimates offered by research is that leadership is about one-third born and two-thirds made. Research suggests that extraversion is consistently associated with obtaining leadership positions and leader effectiveness. There is also some evidence that being bold, assertive or risk-taking can be advantageous for leaders. Leaders also need to be smart (social intelligence, not IQ) to analyze situations and figure out courses of action. Empathy, or ability to know followers, is also advantageous for leaders (although much of this is learned). The leader must be able to know what followers want, when they want it and what prevents them from getting what they want.

Leaders have to call the shots. They do well when they operate inclusively and obtain input from their team members, but at the end of the day they have to make the difficult decisions.

10 Ways to Become a Better Leader

1. Understand your Leadership Style

What are your strengths? Which area may need some improvement? Here is some more information about leadership styles.

Authoritative Leadership

The authoritative leader knows the mission, is confident in working toward it and empowers team members to take charge just as she is. The authoritative leader uses vision to drive strategy and encourages team members to use their strengths and emerge as leaders themselves.

The authoritative leader provides high-level direction, but she lets those she leads figure out the best way to get there. Authoritative leaders are always striving for progress. They inspire others to adopt a similar attitude.

When the authoritative leadership style works best

An authoritative team leadership is not restrictive. It propels advancements when:

- A leader is truly competent to take charge
- Detailed instructions are not required
- Employees already have the tools they need to do their most effective work

Those who adopt an authoritative leadership style when they don't have the appropriate experience, or when they try to wield authority over others in an aggressive way, will fail. An authoritative leader must be confident and have the experience to back it up in order to be successful.

Transactional Leadership

A transactional leader may be in a position of leadership, such as in a managing role, but this leader is not necessarily one to embrace going above and beyond what is expected. The transactional leader dangles a carrot in front of each work-horse. If the employee does something positive, they are rewarded. If they don't meet the exact expectation, they may be punished.

This type of task-oriented leadership focuses on meeting basic expectations. The transactional leader may decide roles and ways to monitor performance so that results are delivered. But encouraging innovation isn't as prevalent with this type of leadership style.

When the transactional leadership style works best

Transactional leadership may be appropriate when:

- You are working with team members who are new to a certain type of project or need detailed guidance
- Clear goals and a plan to get there will increase productivity
- The team will benefit from celebrating victories together or holding each other accountable when someone doesn't do the work they're supposed to

The downside to transactional leadership is that this type of style focuses on the work, not the people. Employees want to feel like their work has a broader purpose and want to meaningfully connect with work. Transactional leadership doesn't foster the human-work connection.

Servant Leadership

Servant leaders get in the trenches with their team. Their goal is to achieve the best outcome. To do that, these types of leaders make themselves available to help with issues, work alongside those they manage and develop those they manage into better employees.

Servant leaders coach. They're willing to stay late and get in early when it's called for, just like everyone else. Servant leaders are focused on constantly transforming their teams into stronger, more efficient, more productive and happier entities. Servant leaders are empathetic and use emotional intelligence to guide their leadership decisions.

When the servant leadership style works best

You might want to employ a servant leader mindset when:

- A team is in desperate need of a great example to look up to and learn from
- A team has conflict and needs mending
- Big projects require all hands-on deck

Servant leadership can have many positive outcomes, but it's also time-consuming. Servant leaders must also be aware that they need to avoid doing all the work. When they give *too* much of themselves, they don't give team members as much of a chance to learn. That can create inefficiencies and missed opportunities to lead in other areas.

Democratic Leadership

Just like a political democracy, where people with diverse opinions work together to come up with a consensus for decisions, a democratic leader gets everyone involved. The whole team is a part of creating a vision and the ideal way to get there. Democratic leaders embrace group meetings and surveys. They value transparency in decision-making. They want their team to feel as involved in work processes as they are.

Employees who work for a democratic leader are aware that they're part of a larger team. They learn the value of collaboration and know they play a role in the evolution of their work environment. Democratic leaders foster discussion, but they also are able to step in when needed and make decisions that's guided by overall input.

When the democratic leadership style works best

A democratic leadership style could help teams when:

- A new project that will benefit from brainstorming is introduced
- There is a problem to tackle, and fresh ideas are needed.
- Tight-knit, highly collaborative teams are in the formation stage, like those at startups or new small businesses

Using this type of democratic, team leadership theory on a constant basis can have drawbacks, though. A leader who never really takes charge and instead lets everyone else debate every decision can lose respect as an authority. Team members may not understand why they're even reporting to someone who only leads in a democratic style in the workplace.

Empathetic Leadership

The empathetic leader recognizes that great work starts with engaged workers. This type of leader strives to create strong emotional bonds within a team so that those working on it feel a sense of belonging. The empathetic leader makes it a priority to have teammates satisfied with them as a manager and with their team. The empathetic leader focuses on people first, then work.

Empathetic leaders aren't micromanagers. They empower team members to do their work, and offer themselves up as a resource whenever their team members need them. They're quick to dole out praise and offer support when needed.

When the empathetic leadership style works best

Empathetic leadership can be effective when:

- A competent team knows the job they need to do and how to effectively execute it
- Little direction is needed from the leader
- The team will benefit more from space and independence to complete tasks than micromanaging

An empathetic leader who only focuses on the people and not the work, though, can leave employees confused and unmotivated. With no clear direction, a hands-off approach to work-related leadership can lead to mistakes, inefficiencies and poor results.

Narcissistic Leadership: The Style to Avoid

One type of leadership that is best avoided in most work situations is the narcissistic leader, also known as a coercive leader. Instead of empowering team members to work toward the best possible outcome, the narcissistic leader has an agenda and aims to coerce those they're leading to carry it out.

Narcissistic traits

Narcissistic leadership is self-centered. It's not often results-focused, and it is disrespectful to the team. This type of leader doesn't lead – he dictates.

Leadership should foster collaboration and intrinsic motivation. A narcissistic leader who lacks empathy will instead breed disinterest or resentment.

There is one exception to when a narcissistic leadership style may be appropriate – when quick action is needed to avert a crisis, like a battlefield situation. But in the workplace, be aware when narcissistic leadership traits are emerging. Try to avoid those actions.

Find the Most Effective Leadership Style for You

If you recognize that there is one type of leadership style that dominates your work style, look for opportunities to put other leadership styles into practice when they're appropriate.

If you haven't connected with your team members on a personal level, put on your empathetic leader hat and have some one-on-ones where you get to know each team member's perceived strengths and career goals. If you've taken a more hands-off approach to leadership, think about future projects where being more vocal can enhance the results.

Shifting your leadership style based on the situation or team member you're dealing with doesn't make you inconsistent. It can make you more successful, because you can connect more effectively and guide your team toward better results.

2. Encourage Creativity

Intellectual stimulation is one of the leadership qualities that defines transformational leadership. Followers need to be encouraged to express their creativity. Effective leaders should offer new challenges with ample support to achieve these goals.

One way to foster creativity is to offer challenges to group members, making sure that the goals are within the grasp of their abilities. The purpose of this type of exercise is to get people to stretch their limits, but to not become discouraged by barriers to success.

3. Serve as a Role Model

Great leaders exemplify the behaviors and characteristics that they encourage in their followers. They walk the walk and talk the talk. As a result, group members admire these leaders and work to emulate these behaviors. If you want to become a better leader, work on modeling the qualities that you would like to see in your team members.

4. Be Passionate

Would you look to someone for guidance and leadership if they did not truly care about the goals of the group? Of course not! Great leaders are not just focused on getting group members to finish tasks; they have a genuine passion and enthusiasm for the projects they work on. You can develop this leadership quality by thinking of different ways you can express your zeal. Let people know that you care about their progress. When one person shares something with the rest of the group, be sure to tell them how much you appreciate such contributions.

5. Listen and Communicate Effectively

Focus on providing one-on-one communication with group members. Good leaders should express sincere care and concern for the members of their group both verbally and non-verbally. By keeping the lines of communication open, these leaders can ensure that group members feel able to make contributions and receive recognition for their achievements.

6. Have a Positive Attitude

Have an upbeat, optimistic attitude that serves as a source of inspiration for followers. If leaders seem discouraged or apathetic, members of the group are likely to also become uninspired. Even when things look bleak and your followers start to feel disheartened, try to stay positive. This does not mean viewing things through rose-colored glasses. It simply means maintaining a sense of optimism and hope in the face of challenges.

7. Encourage People to Make Contributions

Let the members of your team know that you welcome their ideas. Leaders who encourage involvement from group members are often referred to as democratic or participative leaders. While they retain the final say over all decisions, they encourage team members to take an active role in producing ideas and plans. Research has shown that using a democratic leadership style leads to greater commitment, more creative problem-solving and improved productivity.

8. Motivate your Followers

Great leaders provide inspirational motivation to encourage their followers to get into action. Of course, being inspirational isn't always easy. Fortunately, you don't need motivational speeches to rouse your group members. Some ideas for leadership inspiration include being genuinely passionate about ideas or goals, helping followers feel included in the process and offering recognition, praise and rewards for people's accomplishments.

9. Offer Rewards and Recognition

Another important quality of a good leader involves knowing that offering effective recognition and rewards is one of the best ways to help followers feel appreciated and happy. It may also come as no surprise that happy people tend to perform better at work. According to researchers Teresa Amabile and Steven Kramer, leaders can help group members feel happier by offering help, removing barriers to success and rewarding strong efforts.

10. Keep Trying New Things

Who says leadership is a one-way relationship? As you work toward developing some of these leadership qualities, don't forget to look to your followers for feedback an inspiration. Pay attention to the things that have been effective in the past and always be on the lookout for new ways to inspire, motivate and reward group members.

Transformational Leadership

Transformational leadership is a type of leadership style that can inspire positive changes in those who follow and is the kind of leadership necessary in the community-based nonprofit space. Transformational leaders are generally energetic, enthusiastic and passionate. Not only are these leaders concerned and involved in the process; they are also focused on helping every member of the group succeed as well.

Intellectual stimulation, individualized consideration, inspirational motivation and idealized influence are components of transformation leadership.

Intellectual Stimulation

Transformational leaders not only challenge the status quo; they also encourage creativity among followers. The leader encourages followers to explore new ways of doing things and new opportunities to learn.

Individualized Consideration

Transformational leadership also involves offering support and encouragement to individual followers. In order to foster supportive relationships, transformational leaders keep lines of communication open so that followers feel free to share ideas and so that leaders can offer direct recognition of the unique contributions of each follower.

Inspirational Motivation

Transformational leaders have a clear vision that they are able to articulate to followers. These leaders are also able to help followers experience the same passion and motivation to fulfill these goals.

Idealized Influence

The transformational leader serves as a role model for followers. Because followers trust and respect the leader, they emulate this individual and internalize his or her ideals.

Leadership and management are different

The terms leadership and management are often used interchangeably, but there are key differences between leaders and managers. Leaders and managers bring different behavioral characteristics and different skill sets to their work.

When organizations are dynamic and transforming, people at the top are expected to exhibit leadership. Management has traditionally been used to describe what executives do under conditions of stability.

All nonprofits need leaders and managers. Leadership skills are critical because of the organization's role as a community change agent.

Managers are responsible for ensuring the smooth flow of an organization. They provide guidance, analysis and risk management to their teams. Leaders are charged with inspiring the team and the broader community environment.

Managers ensure that the organization achieves its goals. They analyze the tasks at hand and prioritize them. Because of their knowledge of the strengths and weaknesses of each team member, delegating responsibilities, negotiating conflict that may exist, tracking the workflow and receiving and evaluating the final product. All this must be done as they observe, negotiate and evaluate the workflow.

Conversely, leaders have their eye on the bigger picture. They too are concerned with the organization's ability to achieve its goals, but they are also focused on conceptualizing and articulating a vision that matches the organization's vision for itself and its community.

Leadership has been equated with dynamism, vibrancy and charisma. While management has been equated to hierarchy, equilibrium and control.

Here are some primary distinctions between leaders and managers:

- Leaders lead people. Managers manage processes
- Leaders create and communicate the vision. Managers implement the vision
- Leaders take the first step. Managers take the next step
- Leaders ask "why" and "what." Managers ask "how" and "when"
- Leaders align people. Managers organize people
- Leaders motivate and inspire. Managers administrate and direct
- Leaders mentor, teach and pull the team. Managers coach, show, and push the team
- Leaders challenge the status quo. Managers work with the status quo
- Leaders unleash potential. Managers coordinate resources

In the final analysis, managers cannot be successful without being good leaders and leaders cannot be successful without being good managers.

Six Strategies for Young Nonprofit Employees to Become Next Generation Leaders

Take control of your career

You are in charge of your own career. It is true that your executive director should have your best interests at heart, but don't wait for him/her to mentor you. Take the initiative and ask for opportunities to lead or take on special projects. Offer to lead a staff development effort, facilitate a meeting or present a report to the Board. Find workshops and trainings you wish to attend and ask for support in doing so.

Develop broad management expertise

Look outside your particular area of interest and find ways to broaden your experience. Next generation leaders will need to understand budgeting, grant-writing and how to supervise. Embrace these responsibilities instead of dismissing them as administrative. You will need to be a generalist if you aim to serve as a leader and these areas and skills will put you closer to the heart of the organization. Building management skills while you build programmatic skills will help you overcome the nonprofit tendency to pit program against management.

Join a board

If you haven't done so, you are missing out on an ideal way to prepare yourself for nonprofit leadership. Besides providing great experience, contacts made while on a Board may become mentors or even referrals to new job opportunities.

Find a mentor

A mentor provides a model of career development and he or she can also introduce you to people, provide strategic career advice and help you avoid mistakes. Look around. Who is doing interesting work? Who inspires you? A mentor does not have to be in your organization. Look around at people in your pro-fessional networks and approach likely people and develop a relationship. Someone you ask to mentor you will likely be flattered but don't overwhelm them right away...start with coffee and conversation first.

Work with a coach

Mentors can help you build a network and give advice, but a coach can help you build your skills and develop a career strategy. Executive coaches have existed in the business sector for many years and now that practice is appearing in the nonprofit world as well.

Recognize and respect generational differences

Try this: stop saying they just don't get it. It doesn't matter who is right or wrong, just try to understand generational differences and take the initiative to work over and around them. Remember it may be just as difficult for your older colleagues to understand you. When you recognize these differences, find a way to remember to focus on the work rather than on individuals. Understand that you are all working towards the same goal, but your approaches might be different.

Chapter 7

Show Me the Money: Funding your Work

Funding is the life blood of a nonprofit organization. Having multiple streams of funding is vital for sustainability. KISRA grew organically and I learned grant writing so that I could raise funds for the programs we were developing and to cover my salary so that I did not become a burden to the church. It was my on-the-job training, and I embraced the challenge. Grant writing was not taught in engineering school, but I was a fast learner.

Back in my early KISRA days, I remember writing a grant to the WV Division of Criminal Justice Services. It sounded like it would be perfect for the after-school program. I had received a grant announcement in the mail, and I decided to give it a try. We were not funded. However, Helena Lee, the program administrator, reached out to me to set up a meeting to review the grant requirements. She went through the application with me and explained what was being asked and appropriate responses to the various sections. Her feedback was invaluable. She then encouraged me to apply for a planning grant that was coming due. I took her advice, and that planning grant became our first state government grant. I am grateful to Helena for investing her precious time in me and for the many years of financial and capacity building support we received from the Safe and Drug-Free Communities Program.

Without any formal grant writing training, I wrote all of KISRA's grants and raised over $30 million during my tenure. I wish we had someone else designated as the development director or grant writer, but I started in this role and continued even after the team had grown to more than 60. It was actually difficult to find the funding to hire someone as most of the grants we received were tied to projects. General support funding was limited. I wish we received more unrestricted funding from funding sources like donor-advised and donor-designated which I learned about later in my current career in philanthropy. For one of our larger federal grants, I was able to include the costs of a consultant to assist with the business plan for that particular project.

Many of our early grants at KISRA came from state-governments sources and they were reimbursable. They were for the after-school program operations. At times reimbursements were delayed. There were times when payroll was coming up and there was not enough money in the bank to cover it. But by God's grace, we always made it. The church often served as a guarantor for KISRA and paid my salary until I was able to raise enough grant funding to cover it.

A few definitions before we get into the nitty gritty about financial resources for nonprofit work.

Fundraising: the raising of assets and resources from various sources for the support of an organization or a specific project

Grant: a financial donation given to support a person, organization, project or program. Most grants are awarded to nonprofit organizations, with 501(c)(3) designation from the Internal Revenue Service

Solicit: 1a to ask (a person or group) for a contribution of money, resources, a service or opinion. **1b** to request or try to acquire (such a contribution)

Grantor: an entity that gives a grant

Prospect: any potential donor whose linkages, giving ability, and interests have been confirmed

All nonprofit fundraising programs must have three key components – a case for support, leadership and sources. The case for support succinctly presents the reasons why an organization needs and merits philanthropic support. It outlines the organization's programs, current needs and plans. Leadership is essential to chart the course and follow through on commitments. Although following through on your commitments sounds simple, it's a habit that can make or break your credibility as a nonprofit leader. I started as a new, Black nonprofit leader with limited sector experience, working in a poor neighborhood at an organization started by a small church. I earned respect and built trust by keeping my word and following through when I made a commitment. Even though I felt scrutinized by people

with power and resources, I used the challenge as an opportunity to show naysayers what my team and I could achieve
regardless of our circumstances.

There are many fundraising methods available to nonprofits.
They include:
- Personal solicitation
- Telephone solicitation
- Mail solicitation/Direct mail
- Electronic solicitation
- Special events
- Grant proposals
- Earmarks

KISRA received two federal earmarks with the help of
Congresswoman (now Senator) Shelley Moore Capito and
Senator Robert Bird for the Empowerment Center. We received
random personal gifts from people like Nelle Chilton, Newton
Thomas and Ekklesia Ministries. We tried special events like a
Benefit Dinner with Tony Brown, Cooking in the Capital, Soul-
Line Dances, Tea and Tales of Tenacity women empowerment
events, No-Show Holiday Events, but none of them netted significant amounts of funding and they were a lot of extra work
on my already stretched team. So, I spent significant amounts
of my time raising funds through grants and I was successful at
it. When proposals were not funded, I took the time to learn the
reasons why so that I could do better the next time.

One of my greatest disappointments was in 2015 when a high
scoring federal proposal was not funded and I had to terminate

some of our staff. The agency had changed the way they allocated funding to multiple program areas. We were grantees of theirs, but to maintain the level of programming we had in progress we needed two grants to sustain our efforts. There were no rules against this, so I submitted proposals to two program areas in the same agency. Both proposals had scores in the 90s, but only one was funded. This experience highlighted the vulnerability of nonprofits that rely on federal funding.

Federal government agencies usually offer the most significant grants. However, it is essential not to rely on these support sources solely and build local funding relationships. Specific federal government funding streams are often linked to a particular political administration. Be mindful of this as you plan. For example, faith-based initiatives were once in vogue during the George W. Bush administration. One rarely hears this term anymore. KISRA was blessed to be the top recipient in the first federal faith-based grant program in the nation.

Basic grant writing steps

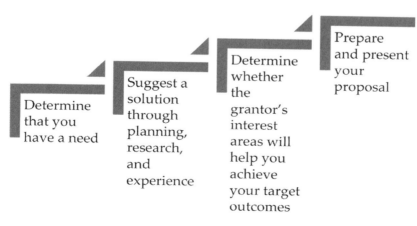

Determine that you have a need

Suggest a solution through planning, research, and experience

Determine whether the grantor's interest areas will help you achieve your target outcomes

Prepare and present your proposal

As the old saying goes, "do not put all of your eggs in one basket." Funding fluctuations stress programs and organizations and make it difficult to provide consistent, quality services. High-performing staff may leave or be laid off if funding shortfalls are anticipated. No one likes to be in this kind of environment. This reality emphasizes the need to secure funding from diverse sources to sustain your efforts. Sources could include the following:

- Government entities
- Foundations
- Businesses
- Corporations
- Workplace campaigns
- Service clubs and associations
- Religious organizations
- Events (e.g., galas, golf tournaments, pickleball tournaments, etc.)
- Fees for services/products
- Individuals

Government Entities

Federal, state, county, local government and agencies fall under the government entities umbrella. These entities need to address pressing social problems. Strategies for building relationships with these funding sources include:

- design programs of specific interest to the funding agency
- establish relationships with decision-makers and discuss proposal in advance of submitting

- complete and submit applications thoroughly and in a timely way
- engage local advocates
- meet with public officials responsible for funding agency
- be patient - obtaining government support can take time
- attend information sessions
- follow agencies of interest on social media

I was able to establish great connections to government entities to fund KISRA's work. These sources included, AmeriCorps, Kanawha County Schools-Pre-K, Justice Assistance, Mayor's Office of Economic and Community Development, Office of Economic Opportunity, Strategic Prevention Framework State Incentive Grant, US Department of Education-Safe & Drug-Free Communities, US Department of Health and Human Services-Assets for Independence, US Department of Health and Human Services- Office of Community Services, US Department of Justice – Second Chance Act, US Department of Housing and Urban Development - Economic Development Initiative, US Department of Housing and Urban Development - Housing Counseling Program, US Department of Agriculture, US Department of Housing and Urban Development- Rural Housing and Economic Development, US Small Business Administration, Workforce WV - Governor's Set Aside, WV Alliance for Sustainable Families, WV Budget Digest, WV Division of Criminal Justice Services - Juvenile Justice Delinquency Prevention, WV Department of Health and Human Resources - Behavioral Health and Health Facilities, WV Department of Health and Human Resources - REACH WV, WV Department of Health and Human Resources

- Family Planning, WV Department of Health and Human Resources — Promoting Responsible Education Program, WV Housing Development Fund, West Virginia University Extension and West Virginia State University.

Most federal grants are listed on the www.grants.gov website. I encourage you to search this site regularly and set up alerts so that you can track grants of interest. Grantstation is another invaluable source of grant information.

Over 75 percent of KISRA's funding came from government entities. A federal grant from the US Department of Health and Human Services, Administration for Children and Families, Office of Family Assistance was KISRA's largest grant. We were awarded $13.6 million over 10 years. This particular funding source helped us to build our capacity and grow the organization. It even got me recognition from President Barack Obama as a champion of change. The recognition press release is below:

THE WHITE HOUSE
Office of Communications
FOR IMMEDIATE RELEASE
June 11, 2012

White House Highlights Dr. Michelle Mickle Foster as a Fatherhood "Champion of Change"

WASHINGTON, DC — On Wednesday, June 13th, the White House Office of Public Engagement and Office of Faith-Based and Neighborhood Partnerships will honor Dr. Michelle Mickle

Foster as one of ten individuals who are doing tremendous work in the field of fatherhood and are addressing the needs low-income men and boys.

"These Champions of Change do great work to promote responsible fatherhood in communities all across the country," said Michael Strautmanis, White House Deputy Assistant to the President. "All of us have a stake in forming stronger bonds between fathers and their children and today's event will celebrate the great joy, responsibility, and work of raising healthy children."

"Today's Fatherhood Champions of Change represent some of the best advocates in the field of fatherhood and serving low-income fathers and boys. These Champions know the vital role fathers play in the lives of our children," said Joshua DuBois, the White House Director of the Office of Faith-Based and Neighborhood Partnerships.

The Champions of Change program was created as a part of President Obama's Winning the Future initiative. Each week, a different sector is highlighted and groups of Champions, ranging from educators to entrepreneurs to community leaders, are recognized for the work they are doing to serve and strengthen their communities.

To watch this event live, visit www.whitehouse.gov/live at 1:00 pm ET on June 13th.

Dr. Michelle Mickle Foster is the CEO of the Kanawha Institute for Social Research & Action, Inc. (KISRA) and has served in this capacity since 1998 (14 years). She developed all of KISRA's 13 major programs that are in the areas of education, employment, economic empowerment and behavioral health. Under her leadership, KISRA has grown from one employee sponsored by Ferguson Memorial Baptist Church (KISRA's founder) to a team of over 70 employees with funding from multiple local, state, and federal sources. Dr. Foster and the KISRA team serve and empower thousands of West Virginians annually. Dr. Foster has a doctorate in community economic development and was formerly a chemical engineer.

#

As a part of the recognition, Pastor Emanuel Heyliger (KISRA Board Chair), Carl Chadband (Chief Operations Officer) and I were treated to a tour of the White House. I then represented KISRA on a panel discussion with other Champions of Change from around the country. It was an awesome experience. It was a career highlight, even though I did not get to meet President Obama in person. He did send me a personal letter and autographed photo that I framed and hung in my KISRA office and currently hangs in my office at The Greater Kanawha Valley Foundation.

Other local and national recognition over the years have included the Alpha Phi Alpha Fraternity Impact Award for Service (2022), Women of Achievement Award from the YWCA Charleston (2020); Living the Dream Award from the WV Martin Luther King, Jr. Holiday Commission (2016); Woman on a Mission Award from Union Mission (2016); Civil Rights Day Award from the State of West Virginia, Office of the Governor (2015); Dr. Martin Luther King, Humanitarian Award from the Saint Albans Ministerial Association (2015); Fatherhood Champion of Change recognition from President Barack Obama at the White House (2012); National Association of University Women, Charleston Branch, Leadership Award (2012); Omega Psi Phi Fraternity,

Inc., Theta Psi Chapter, Citizen of the Year (2012); Charleston Police Department, Award for Community Service (2011); U.S. Small Business Administration, Minority Business Champion (2009); and West Virginia State University, President's Award for Community Service (2009).

Foundations

There are four main types of foundations – private, community, corporate/company sponsored and operating. I am currently the president and CEO of a community foundation. Motivations of foundations include community support, sociopolitical concerns, historical roles (like the philanthropic interests of the founders), seed money for new projects, systems change and tax advantages.

Here are some strategies for building relationships with foundations:

- Research the foundation's mission, vision, and priorities usually found on their website
- Analyze the foundation guidelines
- Approach, enquire, and develop personal relationships with grantmaking staff
- Attend foundation sponsored events
- Follow the foundation on social media
- Develop, write and package a letter of inquiry, project summary or request for support

Most foundations can be found on https://www.candid.org If you can't afford a subscription or just want to preview this system, I recommend the public library as a resource. I spent many hours in the Kanawha County Public library in Charleston in my early years at KISRA researching nonprofit operations and grant sources. The internet was not ubiquitous in those days.

Community foundations usually manage donor-advised and donor-designated funds in addition to the discretionary funds available for competitive grants. These donor-directed funds would be listed in the organization's annual report. Do your research and get to know the fundholders and increase their awareness of your program. This may possibly lead to general support for your organization.

Additionally, community foundations house giving circles. In a giving circle, like-minded individuals pool their philanthropic dollars and decide as a group where to distribute them. I am a founding member of the African American Philanthropy in Action giving circle at the Greater Kanawha Valley Foundation. We give our time, talent and treasures to make community impact through nonprofit partners.

The Greater Kanawha Valley Foundation was an early funder of KISRA. They believed in our mission and supported several of our youth initiatives over the years. They even retained KISRA to conduct a needs assessment to inform their place-based funding efforts. While at KISRA, I never imagined that I was destined to be the President and CEO of the Foundation.

Over the years, BB&T Foundation, Bernard McDonough Foundation, Claude Worthington Benedum Foundation, Dow Foundation, Mary Reynolds Babcock Foundation, One Foundation and Verizon Foundation have all supported KISRA.

Businesses

Banks, utility companies, community stores and businesses all fall into this category. Strategies for building relationships with businesses:

- Nominate local business owners/executives for Board
- Establish a local business council
- Seek in-kind support that serves organizational need and then prominently recognize the business and its contribution
- Ask a business to sponsor an aspect of the organization
- Request support for a specific project
- Comb through their website and see how they're engaged in the community to see if they support organizations like yours

Appalachian Power, Bank One/Chase Bank, BB&T Bank, Fifth Third Bank, Suntrust Bank and WesBanco Bank supported KISRA over the years.

Corporations

This category includes direct giving, executive discretionary funds, local site or subsidiary giving, and in-kind gifts such as marketing support, research and development activities or products needed. Strategies for building relationships with corporations:

- Establish relationships with employees: invite them to be Board and committee members, etc.
- Develop compelling reasons for corporate support that tie to the corporation's mission, vision and priorities
- Inquire / approach / qualify / discuss interests
- Comb through their website and see how they're engaged in the community to see if they support organizations like yours
- Great corporate citizens are usually engaged in supporting the community in some way, so some online research to discover their niche

Workplace campaigns

The United Way is an example of a workplace campaign. Workplace campaigns bestow member-agency status on a nonprofit, leading to annual allocations. Some make discretionary grants for various community-developed projects. While others sponsor donor-option programs allowing individual employees to make on-the-job contributions.

Workplace campaigns want to demonstrate their role as a good community partner. Through payroll deductions, they provide an efficient way for people to make donations with encouragement of supervisors

Strategies for building relationships with workplace campaigns:

- Join the local federation as a member agency
- Apply for discretionary grants

- Seek participation in a federated donor-option program - either an existing one or a new one made up of similar organizations

Clubs and associations

Clubs and associations include service clubs, social clubs and trade associations. Each club has specific interests which could include community source and business or social concerns of members. Strategies for building relationships with clubs and associations:

- Identify potential support in the community
- Join the organization if appropriate, or approach through a member
- Discover ways to educate the group about the cause and why it warrants their support
- Offer appropriate things for the group, e.g., meeting space, speakers, etc.
- Offer to host a business after hours event

I am currently a member of the Charleston Rotary Club. Over the years the club has supported a number of local initiatives and has even mobilized other philanthropic partners to rebuild a community playground.

Religious organizations

Religious organizations are concerned about the public good, they are charitable and compassionate, and giving is a part of their ministry to the community. Strategies for building relationships with religious organizations include:

89

- Make initial connections locally, perhaps through staff or Board of organization
- Determine and articulate a connection between needs and religious organization
- Approach targeted congregation/community through clergy or recognized lay leadership
- If local support not available, inquire about regional or national denomination support; ask for a personal contact to approach
- Always respect these sources' religious motivations for giving
- Inquire about opportunities to speak to church members about your organization

Ferguson Memorial Baptist Church founded KISRA, which was originally a vision of Pastor Emanuel Heyliger. The church invested in me to develop the organization from infancy to adulthood when it could stand on its own. They also purchased an old nightclub in the neighborhood near the church and transformed it into the organization's headquarters – the Empowerment Center. KISRA services were housed in the church until renovations were completed. KISRA would not have existed if it were not for the church.

Events

Special events are social engagements that bring together people from the organization and community to raise awareness of a need, awareness of an organization, and support for a cause. Events include runs/walks, dinners, galas, golf tournaments, etc.

They are labor intensive and when you are an emerging non-profit netting a significant amount of money can be challenging.

Fees for services/products

In my early KISRA years, I was uncomfortable charging for anything. However, I later realized that charging a modest fee when appropriate, increased the perceived value of the product or service. It's also a sustainability strategy.

Nonprofits should always look for opportunities to garner fees for services in line with their core missions. At KISRA we operated some of our initiatives as social enterprises. Social enterprises are businesses whose primary purpose is the common good. They are focused on social, cultural, community economic and/or environmental outcomes and earning revenue. Social enterprises use the methods and disciplines of business and the power of the marketplace to advance their social, environmental and human justice agendas.

Social enterprises produce higher social returns on investment than other models and have a triple bottom line:
1. People/Social
2. Planet/Environmental
3. Profit/Economic

We attempted several social enterprises at KISRA. The first one, the Harambee Child Development Center, was established in 2004, on the first floor of a former nightclub. Initial funding for the center came from the US Department of Health and

Human Services - Office of Community Services, a congressional appropriation secured with the help of Congresswoman (now Senator) Shelley Moore Capito, the State of West Virginia and the Greater Kanawha Valley Foundation. Nurturing, certified staff provided quality childcare for over 70 children and 20 jobs were created.

The KISRA Micro-Loan Program was established in 2009. After a lengthy approval process, loan funds were secured from the US Small Business Administration and the Claude Worthington Benedum Foundation. Loans up to $50,000 were made to small business owners. Technical assistance, including business planning and operations training, were provided as well. One KISRA job was created and over 20 jobs were created by borrowers.

KISRA Paradise Farms was established in 2013. This urban farm gave residents access to fresh, organic produce for a healthier lifestyle. Responsible Fatherhood and Second Chance program participants received farm skills training to build their resumes. Initial funding for this enterprise came from US Department of Health and Human Services - Office of Family Assistance and JP Morgan Chase Foundation. Seven permanent jobs and multiple transitional jobs for program participants were created.

Finally, a culinary enterprise was established in 2013 with initial funding from US Department of Health and Human Services - Office of Family Assistance. It incorporated culinary skills training in a commercial kitchen, a professional catering service and a mobile kitchen in a food truck. This enterprise created three jobs.

Planning for funding sustainability should be a strategic process that addresses the long-term needs of a program and organization. Your funding sources to meet your annual operations budget will need adjustments based on changing trends in economic and political cycles. Therefore, a defined fundraising plan with an adaptive timeframe that maintains critical infrastructure is essential for success. See Appendix E for a sample fundraising plan that I have used over the years.

Chapter 8
Tell Your Story: Control Your Narrative

In my 18-year career at KISRA we were about supporting families from every walk of life, ever since being started by Ferguson Memorial Baptist Church in 1993. We were about creating stronger families. Better educated families. More empowered families, ready to change the course of their lives and contribute to our community. It all started with the desire to help children. It grew to become a comprehensive offering of programs that HEAL and benefit people from every walk of life in several West Virginia counties.

The very first program was the Harambee Learning Center, in our Learning division. The center provided area children with an after-school program that offered help with homework, mentoring, enrichment, recreational activities and more. After opening the center in 1998, we soon realized that many of the children faced risk factors including academic failure, extreme economic deprivation and exposure to alcohol and drugs. It was apparent that our community needed additional services to strengthen families.

We quickly developed the Employment and Asset Development divisions and the programs within them. We worked with TANF

(Temporary Assistance to Needy Families) recipients, offering them workforce readiness training and job placement assistance. We also reached out to other low- and moderate-income residents, offering them financial counseling because many of them had credit problems. Housing counseling, homebuyer education and home construction were also added.

We saw that residents needed childcare, so we opened the Harambee Child Development Center in 2004, which created more jobs in an economically deprived community. We started helping residents become more financially self-sufficient through KISRA Works! Our self-sufficiency and asset development strategies also led to the establishment of a matched savings program and a business loan program.

Because so many of these families were headed by single mothers, we began helping men become better fathers and providers through our Pathways to Responsible Fatherhood Initiative in 2003. And because the majority of that program's participants had criminal backgrounds, we established our Second Chance Mentoring Program.

We saw that our mental health facilities were overcrowded so we created our Health division. We began befriending and supporting mental health patients so that they could remain at home. And because children get the best head start when they come into the world wanted, we opened our Family Planning Clinic in 2011 and expanded it to a full-service community clinic in 2012.

We realized that because of their troubled backgrounds the parents completing our responsible fatherhood and second chance programs were having difficulty finding employment. So, we established the Growing Jobs Project in 2013 to alleviate some of these challenges. The project included urban farming (Paradise Farms), agriculture and culinary skills training, a food truck and catering service and a food hub to create jobs.

The above narrative captures the story of KISRA, the organization I led from 1998 to 2016 - a grassroots, faith-motivated initiative that grew and evolved as community needs were identified. Be available to tell your story and control the narrative about your program and organization. Often, nonprofit leaders are so swamped doing the work and addressing needs that they forget to pause and tell their stories. I know from experience that this is often difficult to balance, but it should be a priority. Here are three tips for telling your story.

Cast a Big Vision. Your nonprofit may only be working in a tiny corner of a small town, but for the people you serve, your work is life changing. When telling your nonprofit story, show people the lives you have changed, the outcomes you have achieved and the work that would be possible if you had more resources at your disposal. KISRA is located in an unincorporated, impoverished area in West Virginia. However, we did not let our condition minimize our aspirations to meaningfully impact lives.

Appeal to Core Human Values. Regardless of our differences, we all care about the same things: safety, freedom, good health and a better life for our children. So, in addition to showcasing the features of your work, such as the number of people assisted or the number of hot meals you serve each day, focus on the benefits of your work—the core human values. The best way to do this is to make sure stakeholders understand the big picture about your work. For example, if your nonprofit is providing food assistance, be sure to tell stakeholders that you are preventing families from starving and allowing them to live healthy, comfortable lives. Yes, you can tell stakeholders about your programs, but be sure they understand the big vision behind your work: to keep families fed and healthy.

Use Real Examples and Outcomes. Statistics and outcomes do have their place in your nonprofit's story, but primarily as support for your overall, big picture vision focused on one or more core human values. When using statistics and discussing outcomes, one of the best things you can do is to put a face on the numbers by relating them to real-life examples and stories about your work. For example, if you are telling stakeholders about the number of scholarships you gave out this past year, highlight the story of someone who received your scholarship. Nonprofit communications build an emotional connection with the donor. Real-world examples, stories and outcomes are a great way to show how your work has changed lives.

There are multiple avenues for sharing your story. They include social media, videos, website, newspapers (including opinion pieces), newsletters, email marketing, etc. Finally, if you can't afford full-time marketing or communications staff, consider partnering with a university for a fellow or intern to assist you.

Chapter 9
Build Partnerships and Community Support

Partnership is not a posture, but a process - a continuous process that grows stronger each year as we devote ourselves to common tasks. John F. Kennedy

At my core I am shy and introverted. But as a leader, I realized that I can't just stay in my office with my head down, all day, every day. Getting out and being a part of the community is important. I'm a Rotarian and a member of several local and regional philanthropy groups and service organizations and sit on various Boards. I attend business after hours events and various fundraisers and galas not because I have free time on my hands, but because it's what is necessary for me to be in community. The community I am referring to is the fellowship with others who share common attitudes, interests and goals. I am in community with all the people working to make West Virginia an even better place to live, work, play, pray and raise a family. So, I press through my introverted ways and connect to build social capital which I'm defining simply as the existence of a certain set of informal values or norms shared among members of a group that permit cooperation among them.

A partnership is the cooperative relationship between two or more parties for the benefit of both or the greater good. They are formed between individuals, organizations, agencies, foundations, businesses, etc. that want to combine forces for a better result. Partnerships can leverage, to name just a few things, time, money and personnel for a larger impact. They are mutually beneficial to the participating organizations as well as the community as a whole.

Cultivating connections between a program and community stakeholders are key to success. A nonprofit cannot exist on an island by itself. Partnerships build synergy. Synergistic outcomes result from the effectiveness of leadership, administration, management, the efficiency of the alliance, and the sufficiency of resources. A synergistic collaboration involves:

- recruiting a broad range of stakeholders to the group
- motivating participants to work together by articulating common goals
- empowering the group with a collaborative process to address problems
- encouraging group members to develop relationships with one another and engage in an ongoing discourse (Lasker & Weiss, 2003)

Partners play an important role in sustainability and success in several ways:

1. They can connect an organization to more significant resources or expertise. They can also complement an organization's services and serve as an advocate.

2. Partners can help rally the community around an initiative and its desired outcomes.
3. Partners can be an organization's champions and help to tell its story.

I recommend developing a strategic partnership approach with partners across sectors, including alliances among private, public and philanthropic organizations, not when you need them for a funding proposal but as you design your program. For example, one of the most extensive nonprofit programs I ran was a responsible fatherhood program. Our partners included: the Federal Funding Agency; State Division of Corrections and Rehabilitation; State Workforce Offices; State Child Support Enforcement Offices; Churches; 2-year and 4-year Colleges and Universities; Career and Technical Colleges; and Employers.

There are usual partnerships and unusual partnerships. **Usual** partnerships are those that by definition of the problem or issue being addressed have a natural affinity. They are fairly straightforward in composition, but not necessarily easy to create. They include partnerships among training organizations and the job placement service. **Unusual** partnerships are relationships among organizations that at first glance do not share a common purpose. They require more creativity and thinking but often yield even greater results. Unusual partnerships are created when organizations examine their larger interests and the larger interests of others and see the connections and synergy that could be created together.

Both approaches make sense, but they are not easy to do. Building strategic partnerships means:

- Giving up some control
- Rethinking competition for funds
- Being willing to share the limelight on success and failure

At KISRA, I used a simple Memorandum of Understanding to outline partner responsibilities. Refer to Appendix F for a sample MOU.

Chapter 10
Funding Relationships: Developing and Maintaining Them

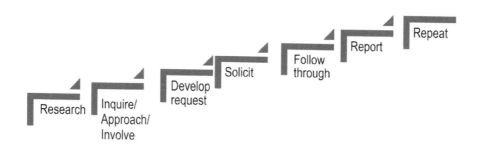

Developing Relationships Step 1: Research

- Identify organizational prospects through online searches and the public library
- Be thorough, but don't let research become an obstacle to personal contact and cultivation of an organizational source; remember people give to people
- Get specific information for each identified prospect – priorities, geographic focus, funding cycles
- Narrow your prospects to sources whose giving guidelines match your organization's needs
- Develop a funding source ranking sheet (and rank your prospects)

Developing Relationships Step 2: Inquire, approach and involve

This may take many forms, depending on the source:

- A letter of inquiry or an email to a foundation or corporate giving office
- A personal call to the local organization
    - o After this initial approach, determine an appropriate and effective way to involve/cultivate the source (e.g., invite a foundation program officer for a site visit, etc.)
- An invitation to the local club president to join your Board or a committee (e.g., involvement)

Developing Relationships Step 3: Develop Request

- Define a project or other funding opportunity that most effectively matches the organization's funding objectives and guidelines with your mission and needs
- Develop the case statement. Remember: what you might state in your case statement to a corporation could be different for government entities, etc. You may need to customize depending on your prospect
- Write a proposal based on the case statement
- Before writing a grant proposal, write a letter of inquiry or project summary to the grant source whether or not it is required
    - o It can save time if the project and the funder are not a good fit. Include an outline / summary of

the proposed project so the organization can respond appropriately
- Determine the timing of the request

Developing Relationships Step 4: Solicit

- If possible, find out who the decision-maker is
- Make "the ask" in the way most appropriate for the source: a proposal, personal call, etc.
- The goal is to motivate individuals from the foundation (or other entity) to invest in your organization, rather than just make a one-time donation
- Consider whether meeting with the funding organization's Board members is appropriate, possible and/or expected of applicants
- Depending on the links to your organization, refer them back to the case statement and the overall organizational case

Developing Relationships Step 5: Follow through

- Follow up on your solicitation to make sure all is in order
- Offer more information or a personal visit, if necessary
- After the gift is received, acknowledge it in writing and keep the organizational source appropriately involved in your organization

Developing Relationships Step 6: Report

- Some organizational sources of support will have reporting procedures; others will leave it open
- Whatever the policy, always report to the funder in an honest, thorough and timely way

Developing Relationships Step 7: Repeat

- Never let this cultivation/reporting/regular contact process stop with an organizational source of support
- Look for the next step in every step you take, plan ahead
- Build transformational relationships, not transactional episodes:
  - o Avoid slipping into an "us vs. them" mentality
  - o Approaching an organization for funding should be viewed as a potential partnership or team working together for a common goal
- Use tailored approaches for unique audiences, no one size fits all

What do funders look for? (Foundations' Perspective)
Since February 2016, I have been serving as the President and CEO of the Greater Kanawha Valley Foundation. These are the elements foundations like ours consider when reviewing proposals:
- Does the organization's mission match our priorities?
- Does the project match our priorities?

- Is the proposal written well? Is it clear, descriptive, logical, free of jargon and well organized?
- Is the project stated in terms of serving the clients/participants? Is it serving marginalized people?
- Does the organization have experience serving the target population?
- Was it developed with client/participant input?
- Does it build on strengths and opportunities as opposed to only focusing on problems and needs?
- Is the project reasonable and doable?
- Do the goals/desired outcomes, methods and evaluation flow from one to the next? Does the organization have the capacity to carry it out?
- What are our impressions regarding the management and reputation of the organization?
- Is there evidence of solid Board and community support and involvement?
- Is there a functioning Board in place?
- Are partnerships or collaborations involved?
- Does the budget tell the same story as the proposal narrative?
- Are there any unexplained amounts on the budget?
- Is the budget sufficient to perform the task?
- Does the budget add up? Is it mathematically, correct?
- Are other funders supporting the work? What percentage of the total project budget is being requested?
- Is the organization current on payroll taxes and other required filings?
- What stories do the IRS Form 990 and financial audit tell?
- Is it clear what the foundation is being asked to fund?

- Is sustainability addressed? Does the applicant have a solid, diversified fundraising plan in place and are they working towards self-sufficiency?
- Do foundation staff or review committee members have personal experience or connections that can add insight?
- Is diversity, equity and inclusion addressed?
- Does the applicant show that they are well-suited to address community need based on history, experience and data?
- Is the project timeline thorough and well developed?
- Do project activities lead to relevant outcomes that are measurable?
- Does the project show creativity and deep-thinking? Is it building upon techniques that work through measurable impact?
- If curriculum is included, is it evidence based?

Why proposals are denied

Understanding the reasons why proposals are denied will help you to achieve success and better manage your precious time in your fund development pursuits. Here are some common reasons:

- The proposal doesn't meet funder priorities. Your grant request should be within the grantor's areas of interest. For example, if a funder doesn't support animal rescue shelters, do not waste your time submitting a proposal for this kind of a project.
- The organization is outside the funder's geographic area. All funders have geographical limitations. Do not waste

your time submitting a proposal to a funder who does not fund in your city, county or state.

- The proposal doesn't follow the format prescribed by the funder. Some funders are even specific about font size and type, margins, line spacing and the number of words. Funders give you a format for a reason. They usually have evaluation metrics aligned with the format. They have limited time to review proposals and are often swamped. Help them to help you by laying out your proposal exactly the way they ask.

- The proposal is poorly written and/or lacks clarity. Remember the KISS principle and keep your proposal simple, straightforward, and succinct. Use spell check and tools like Grammarly to assist as you craft your proposal.

- The proposal's budget is not within funding range. If the funder shares a funding ceiling, do not let your budget exceed it. You are wasting your time if you do.

- The proposing organization is unknown to the funder. Foundations are reluctant to provide significant amounts of financial support to unknown organizations unless it's a special capacity building initiative. Before even submitting a proposal, consider building a relationship with the funder. Share your vision. Be transparent. Share your passion for your work. Ask for help.

Some grantors give you the opportunity to submit a draft proposal and then provide you with feedback. Always incorporate the feedback that you receive. Remember, they are only trying to increase the likelihood of your proposal being approved.

Chapter 11

Grant Proposal Preparation: Everything You Need to Know

It's important to plan before delving into your proposal. Here are some documents to always keep on-hand:

- Mission statement
- Vision statement
- Short description of the organization's services
- Founding date and major historical milestones
- Name and contact information for the CEO and the Board president/chair
- Annual organizational budget
- Sources of funding
- Number of paid staff and number of volunteers
- List of Board members with affiliations, demographics and contact information
- A one-page bio for each key staff member and volunteer
- Job descriptions
- The organization's tax-exempt document
- A current organizational budget
- A current financial statement
- The last two audited financial statements
- Most recent IRS Form 990

- The organization's diversity, equity and inclusion statement
- An organizational chart
- Newspaper clippings or internet links to news coverage about your organization or program
- Program promotional materials and website address
- Stories of impact

You can develop a strong proposal by considering the following:
- Mission, goals, and objectives (outcomes) of the organization
- The initial idea for the project
- An assessment of the need for the project and your organization's capability to undertake it
- Your experience providing similar services or a pilot project
- Phases and alternative approaches to the project
- Gathering required information and building support/involvement from stakeholders
- Planning and scheduling the proposal-writing process, including who is to be involved

Funders may use different terminology, but these are the key elements of a proposal:

Summary or Abstract - Highlights the main points of the proposal and engages the audience that will read it. Remember the need is never about objects; it is about the people being served and what they need.

Problem or Needs Statement – This is the purpose of the request for funding. It is a statement of need and target population. Always use the most current statistics that is specific to your target area as you describe the problem. The statement should include other documented work done to alleviate the problem and what the proposed project hopes to achieve. In includes expected results of project, relationship to other projects in the organization and collaborative relationships to be pursued as part of the project.

Project Goals, Objectives, and Target Outcomes – Remember the SMART acronym. Objectives or desired outcomes should be **S**pecific, **M**easurable, **A**ttainable/**A**chievable, **R**elevant, and **T**ime bound. I highly recommend using a logic model as a program design tool. Refer to Chapter 12 for more about logic models.

Methodology/Activities – What will you do to achieve your desired outcomes? When will the activities occur? Will curriculum be used? Who will administer and staff the project and what are their qualifications and experience? Where will the project be housed?

Evaluation – This element should outline how the project will be measured against the desired outcomes and how a baseline for evaluation will be established if none exists.

A grant-funded project can be evaluated by:
- Feedback from recipients of project services
- Improvements to be made if the project is repeated

- Reduction of problems, either quantitatively or qualitatively
- Attendance at or participation in the project
- An independent evaluation
- Frequency and type of reporting to grantor

I recommend developing an evaluation plan. Refer to Chapter 12 for more about evaluation.

Budget – Always use the format the grantor specifies. The budget should match the project objectives and methodology. Be clear about how the requested amount of funds will fit into the budget and what other funds are supporting the project. Include a narrative to explain and justify budget items. Matching funds (cash and in-kind support) are always great to show, regardless of whether the grantor requires it. Typical budget items include salary and benefits (including payroll taxes), travel, supplies, printing and copying, equipment, communication, materials, evaluation, rent and utilities and indirect expenses.

Sustainability – Sustainability capacity is the ability to maintain an initiative and its benefits over time. According to the Brown School of Social Work at Washington University in St. Louis, program sustainability includes funding stability, partnerships, organizational capacity, program evaluation, program adaptation, communications, environmental support and strategic planning. Developing a plan that includes all of these elements and executing it will show that your organization is on track to making positive impact. Refer to Chapter 19 for more about sustainability.

Supporting Materials – Grantors may ask for photos, quotes, stories of impact, etc. Always be ready with this information.

Finally, always respond directly to the questions posed in each section of the grant application. Copying from old proposals is common. I did this all the time. However, be sure to tweak as needed for each specific grantor. Don't just copy and paste blindly.

Check Appendix I for an example of proposal that was funded for a project at KISRA.

Chapter 12

Evaluate Your Efforts: Measure Your Impact

Everything that can be counted doesn't necessary count; everything that counts cannot necessarily be counted. Albert Einstein

Program evaluation is the use of social research methods to systematically investigate the effectiveness of social intervention programs in ways that are adapted to their political and organizational environments and are designed to inform social action to improve social conditions. (Rosso, Lipsey, Freeman, 2004) Simply put, program evaluation is assessing program operations and results to determine effectiveness and impact. If you aren't achieving the results you expect based on your program design, changes may be necessary. Program evaluation helps keep a program on track with desired outputs and outcomes.

Myths about Evaluation

I would like to debunk some of the myths pertaining to evaluation.

Myth#1: Evaluation is scientific and must be done only by experts
Truth: Evaluation is systematic and can be done by anyone.

Myth #2: Evaluation plans require you to evaluate all programs

Truth: In an ideal world you would have the time and resources to evaluate all programs. In the real world, we all have to pick and choose.

Myth #3: Quantitative data is better than qualitative data

Truth: While quantitative data is an important part of evaluation, some types of information are better communicated through qualitative data. Use both – they are complementary. Match the data collection method to your audience. Qualitative data can help you to capture "the story," which is the most powerful depiction of the benefits of your services.

Myth #4: An evaluation plan must be perfect in order to be effective

Truth: Don't worry about perfection. It's far more important to do something systematically and consistently, than to wait until every last detail has been tested. Be flexible in your design. Allow for change or expansion in midstream if program objectives change or evaluation data shows a new direction for inquiry.

Myth #5: Evaluating only success stories ensures positive evaluations

Truth: An effective evaluation should assess both the positive and negative aspects of the program you are evaluating. You can learn a great deal about a program by understanding its failures, dropouts and missed opportunities – and that understanding will illuminate and improve future programming.

Myth #6: Raw data is useless after an evaluation report is written

Truth: Raw data is the foundation for your evaluation. Hold onto it! It might become useful again as the program continues to develop. Raw data can provide precious information later, and save time and resources when new issues arise.

Uses of Program Evaluations

Program evaluation results can be used in myriad ways. They inform an organization the extent to which outcomes are attained. How will you know if you're making an impact if you don't measure? Results also help practitioners and organizations make informed decisions. If the results you discover during the evaluation are not what you planned, then you may have to change your approach. Finally, results allow organizations to accurately communicate successes and failures to clients, partners, funders and other stakeholders.

Communication is a key sustainability strategy. Communicating externally about your initiative's effectiveness helps the initiative gain greater visibility and builds support from stakeholders. Internally, evidence that an initiative works builds staff buy-in and support from organizational leaders. The more people know and care about your initiative and mission, the more likely they are to support your efforts to continue providing services in the long term.

Collecting data about your initiative's successes and impact is a powerful tool for gaining support and funding. If your evaluation data shows that your initiative is making an important (or irreplaceable) impact, you can make a strong case for why your initiative needs to continue. Even in times of decreased funding, evaluation and monitoring data are key for the pursuit of new funding sources.

The National Council of Nonprofits and its state association network encourage nonprofits to embrace a culture that supports evaluating the difference your nonprofit is making. This requires first identifying "what does success look like?" Then making a plan that will get you there and collecting information along the way to evaluate whether your nonprofit's progress is getting you closer to success. Finally, it's important also to communicate what you are discovering, and use those lessons to continuously improve performance. All of this is referred to variously as, "outcomes measurement," or "performance management," or simply, "evaluation."

Planning your program evaluation

Here are some key considerations before you embark on your program evaluation journey:

- For what purposes is the evaluation being done?
- Who are the audiences for the information from the evaluation?
- What kind of information is needed to make the decision you need to make and/or enlighten your intended audiences?
- From what sources should the information be collected?

- How can that information be collected in a reasonable fashion?
- When is the information needed?
- What resources are available to collect the information?

The Logic Model: A Useful Step in the Planning Process

While at Southern New Hampshire University I learned from Dr. Jolan Rivera how to develop a logic model and it was life changing. My chemical engineering process design brain was ecstatic. Logic models helped me to put all elements of a program into context. It was an extremely useful tool. Federal grantors loved it and knowing how to develop one for a program was a useful asset. I highly recommend using a logic model to guide your program design and evaluation. Refer to the Appendix G for a logic model I created for KISRA.

A logic model is a systematic and visual way to present and share your understanding of the relationships among the resources you have to operate your program, the activities you plan and the changes or results you hope to achieve. The term logic model is frequently used interchangeably with program theory in the evaluation field. Logic models can alternatively be referred to as theory because they describe how a program works and to what end. Refer to the Appendix L for the logic model design guide from the Kellogg Foundation.

A basic logic model

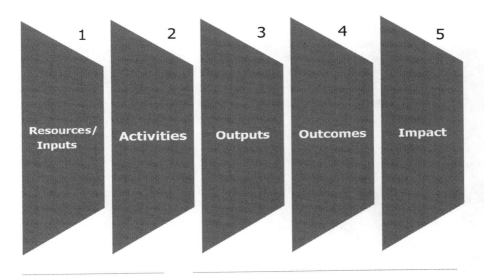

Your Planned Work   Your Intended Results

Sections 1 and 2 comprise your planned work. They describe what resources or inputs you think you need to implement your program and what you intend to do for your program activities

Sections 3, 4 and 5 contain your intended results. Outputs are the direct products of program activities and may include types, levels and targets of services to be delivered by the program. Outcomes are the specific changes in program participants' behavior, knowledge, skills, status and level of functioning. Short-term outcomes should be attainable within 1-to 3-years, while longer-term outcomes should be achievable within a 4-to-6-year timeframe. The logical progression from short-term to long-term outcomes should be reflected in impact occurring within about 7- to-10-years. Impact is the fundamental intended or unintended change occurring in organizations, communities or systems as a result of program activities within 7-to-10 years.

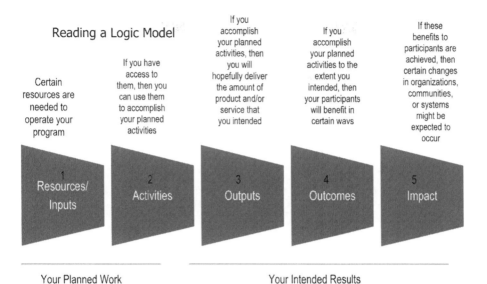

Reading a Logic Model

Certain resources are needed to operate your program

If you have access to them, then you can use them to accomplish your planned activities

If you accomplish your planned activities, then you will hopefully deliver the amount of product and/or service that you intended

If you accomplish your planned activities to the extent you intended, then your participants will benefit in certain ways

If these benefits to participants are achieved, then certain changes in organizations, communities, or systems might be expected to occur

| 1 Resources/ Inputs | 2 Activities | 3 Outputs | 4 Outcomes | 5 Impact |

Your Planned Work | Your Intended Results

Logic Models and Evaluation

Effective evaluation and program success rely on the fundamentals of clear stakeholder assumptions and expectations about how and why a program will solve a particular problem, generate new possibilities and make the most of valuable assets. The logic model approach helps create shared understanding of and focus on program goals and methodology, relating activities to projected outcomes. Many evaluation experts agree that use of the logic model is an effective way to ensure program success. Using a logic model throughout your program helps organize and systematize program planning, management and evaluation functions. Logic models can help craft structure and organization for program design and build in self-evaluation based on shared understanding of what is to take place.

Elements of a Logic Model

Elements of a Logic Model: Resources/Inputs

An input has the following characteristics:

- Describes what resources are needed in order to implement activities
- Expected to be available at the beginning of each activity

Examples of inputs:

- Staff time
- Trainer's time
- Training equipment and materials
- Location
- Transportation
- Lunch

Elements of a Logic Model: Activity

Activities describe specific actions taken during the project. Activities are expected to be completed within the project's "official" timeframe. Activities could be achieved only if the corresponding inputs are available.

Examples of activities could include:

1. Hire instructor
2. Develop/purchase training curriculum
3. Undertake logistical preparations
4. Conduct training
5. Evaluate training

Elements of a Logic Model: Output

Outputs describe what is produced by the project's activities. They are expected to be produced within the project's "official" timeframe. Short-term outcomes could be achieved only if the corresponding outputs are produced.

Outputs are usually numbers of things, like the number of participants served or number of classes hosted.

Elements of a Logic Model: Short-Term Outcome
- Describes change in level of awareness, knowledge and skills of, and/or availability of resources
- Typically achieved within the project's "official" timeframe
- An intermediate outcome could be achieved only if the short-term outcome is attained
- A project typically has more than one short-term outcome

Examples of short-term outcomes:
- Short-term Outcome 1: Acquisition of employable skills
- Short-term Outcome 2: Increased knowledge of financial management and budgeting

Elements of a Logic Model: Intermediate Outcome
- Describes change in behavior that leads people and/or a community to take-action in order to achieve the long-term outcome
- Typically achieved in a period of time that is beyond project's "official" timeframe
- A long-term outcome could be achieved only if the intermediate outcome is attained
- A project typically has one or more intermediate outcomes

Example of an Intermediate Outcome: Improvement in mothers' ability to acquire and maintain gainful employment

Elements of a Logic Model: Long-Term Outcome
- Describes a change in condition
- Usually takes a period of time beyond project's "official" timeframe to achieve it
- Reflects or lead to the organization's mission and vision

Typically, a project has one long-term outcome. It contains:
- *Direction of change*, e.g., "decrease" or "increase"
- *Description of the condition to be changed*, e.g., "economically stable"
- *Persons/groups to be affected by the change*, e.g., "families in Kanawha County"
- *Magnitude of the change*, e.g., "from _% to _%," "number"
- *Timeframe of the change*, e.g., "in _ years," "by the year __"

Elements of a Logic Model: Impact
Impacts are organizational, community, and/or system level changes expected to result from program activities, which might include improved conditions, increased capacity, and/or changes in the policy arena.

Example:
Increase in the number of economically stable families in Kanawha County, West Virginia by at least 700 by the year 2024.

General Categories of Evaluation in Community Development

There are three general categories of evaluation in the community development space – feasibility, formative and summative.

Feasibility occurs prior to program/project development to see if the program/project should be implemented.

Formative is conducted during the development of a project and is aimed at providing information for program improvement, modification and administration. This type of evaluation strengthens or improves the object being evaluated. There are five types of formative evaluation:
1. Implementation evaluation
2. Process evaluation
3. Needs assessment
4. Evaluability assessment
5. Structured conceptualization

Implementation evaluation monitors the fidelity of the program delivery.

Process evaluation investigates the process of delivering the program, including alternative delivery procedures.

Needs assessment determines who needs the program, how great the need is, and what might work to meet the need.

Evaluability assessment determines whether an evaluation is feasible and how stakeholders can help shape its usefulness.

127

Structured conceptualization helps stakeholders define the program, the target population, and the possible outcomes.

Summative evaluation examines the effects or outcomes of some object, summarizing it by describing what happens subsequent to delivery of the program. This type of evaluation assesses whether the object can be said to have caused the outcome, determines the overall impact of the causal factor beyond only the immediate target outcomes and estimates the relative costs associated with the object. Summative (or impact) evaluations are conducted to assess program/project results-outcomes and effectiveness. They are used for purposes of making major decisions about program/project continuation, expansion, reduction and funding.

There are five types of summative evaluation:
1. Outcome evaluation which investigates whether the program caused demonstrable effects on specifically defined target outcomes.
2. Impact evaluation which is broader and assesses the overall or net effects -- intended or unintended -- of the program as a whole.
3. Cost-effectiveness and cost-benefit analysis which address questions of efficiency by standardizing outcomes in terms of their dollar costs and values.
4. Secondary analysis which reexamines existing data to address new questions or use methods not previously employed.
5. Meta-Analysis which integrates the outcome estimates from multiple studies to arrive at an overall or summary judgment on an evaluation question

Outcomes Based Evaluation

Program evaluation with an outcomes focus is increasingly important for nonprofits and asked for by funders. This type of evaluation facilitates you asking if your organization is really doing the right program activities to bring about the outcomes you believe your clients need. Outcomes are benefits to clients from participation in the program.

Steps to accomplishing an outcomes-based evaluation:

1. Identify the major outcomes that you want to examine or verify for the program under evaluation and focus on two to four of them.
2. For each outcome, specify what observable measures, or indicators, will suggest that you're achieving that key outcome with your clients.
3. Specify a "target" goal of clients.
4. Identify what information is needed to show these indicators.
5. Decide how can the information be efficiently & realistically gathered.
6. Analyze and report the findings.

Methods to collect data for evaluation

Surveys

Pros

- Standardization
- Can be designed for electronic completion
- Easy to do with a large group
- Ease of administration

- Ability to tap the "unseen"
- Suitability to tabulation and statistical analysis
- Sensitivity to subgroup differences
- Can be inexpensive
- Sample can be used to provide much information about a population
- Can provide an opportunity for many people to be involved in the decision-making process
- Can be used to record behaviors as well as opinions, attitudes, beliefs and attributes
- Usefulness enhances if combined with other methods, i.e., observation or case study

Cons

- Prone to error
- Requires a separate data-entry step
- More expensive
- Possible "interview evaluation" concern among respondents
- Samples must be carefully selected to ensure statistical meaning
- Subject to misinterpretation, depending on how questions are designed and asked
- Tendency for scope of data to be limited—omission of underlying behavior-al patterns
- Time-consuming compared with less formal methods

Interviews

Pros

- Allows for clarification
- High response rate

- Able to gather in-depth information and to pursue hunches
- Can tailor the line of discussion to the individual
- Easier to reach those who are considered unreachable (the poor, homeless, high status, mobile, etc.)
- May be easier to reach specific individuals (i.e., community leaders, etc.)
- More personalized approach
- Easier to ask open-ended questions, use probes and pick up on nonverbal cues

Cons

- Reactive effect: interviewer's presence and characteristics may bias results
- Expensive
- Requires strong interviewing skills
- Slowest method of data collection and analysis
- Responses may be less honest and thoughtful
- Interviewer should go to location of respondent
- Respondents who prefer anonymity may be inhibited by personal approach
- May reach only a smaller sample
- Difficult to analyze and quantify results

Focus Groups

Pros

- Generate fresh ideas
- Allows clarification
- Efficiency of getting information from a number of people
- Provides immediate sharing and synthesis
- Works well with special participants

- Less expensive and faster than personal interviews
- Personalized approach
- Group members stimulate each other

Cons

- Moderately time consuming
- Moderately expensive
- Subject interpretation
- High cost per participant
- Lack of confidentiality
- Respondents who prefer anonymity may be inhibited by personal approach
- Input may be unbalanced because some group members dominate
- Group members and interviewer can bias responses
- Maybe difficult to analyze or quantify data

Activity Observations
Pros

- Setting is natural, flexible and unstructured
- Evaluator may make his/her identity known or remain anonymous
- Evaluator may actively participate or observe passively
- Can be combined with a variety of other data collection methods
- Generates relevant, quantifiable data
- Most useful for studying a "small unit" such as a classroom

Cons

- Requires skilled observer
- The evaluator has less control over the situation in a natural environment

- Hawthorne effect—if group is aware that they are being observed, resulting behavior may be affected
- Observations cannot be generalized to entire population unless a plan for representativeness is developed
- If observer chooses to be involved in the activity, he/she may lose objectivity
- Not realistic for use with large groups

Selecting Methods

The overall goal in selecting evaluation method(s) is to get the most useful information to key decision makers in the most cost-effective and realistic fashion.

Considerations

- What information is needed to make current decisions about a product or program?
- Of this information, how much can be collected and analyzed in a low-cost and practical manner, e.g., using questionnaires, surveys and checklists?
- How accurate will the information be?
- Will the methods get all of the needed information?
- What additional methods should and could be used if additional information is needed?
- Will the information appear as credible to decision makers, e.g., to funders or top management?
- Will the nature of the audience conform to the methods, e.g., will they fill out questionnaires carefully, engage in interviews or focus groups, let you examine their documentations, etc.?
- Who can administer the methods now or is training required?
- How can the information be analyzed?

Analyzing and Interpreting Information

Analyzing quantitative and qualitative data is often the topic of advanced research and evaluation methods. There are certain basics which can help to make sense of reams of data.

Always start with your evaluation goals. This will help you organize your data and focus your analysis. You can organize data into program strengths, weaknesses and suggestions to improve the program. You could organize data in the chronological order in which clients go through your program. You can categorize data according to the indicators for each outcome.

Basic Analysis of "Quantitative" Information:
- Make copies of your data and store the master copy away.
- Tabulate the information (i.e., add up the number of ratings, rankings, yes's, no's for each question)
- For ratings and rankings, consider computing a mean, or average.
- Consider conveying the range of answers
- (e.g., 20 people ranked "1", 30 ranked "2", and 20 people ranked "3").

Basic Analysis of "Qualitative" Information:
- Read through all the data
- Organize comments into similar categories (e.g., concerns, suggestions, strengths, weaknesses, similar experiences, program inputs, recommendations, outputs, outcome indicators, etc.)
- Label the categories or themes
- Attempt to identify patterns, or associations and causal

relationships in the themes
- Keep all commentary for several years after completion in case needed for future reference

Interpreting the information
1. Attempt to put the information in perspective
2. Consider recommendations to help program staff improve the program, conclusions about program operations or meeting goals, etc.
3. Record conclusions and recommendations in a report document, and associate interpretations to justify your conclusions or recommendations.

Evaluation Plan

Develop an evaluation plan to ensure your program evaluations are carried out efficiently in the future. Funders may want or benefit from a copy of this plan. Ensure your evaluation plan is documented so you can regularly and efficiently carry out your evaluation activities. Record enough information in the plan so that someone outside of the organization can understand what you're evaluating and how.

Please refer to the Appendix H for a Condensed Evaluation Plan

Pitfalls to Avoid

Don't balk at evaluation because it seems far too "scientific." It's not. Usually, the first 20% of effort will generate the first 80% of the plan, and this is far better than nothing.

There is no "perfect" evaluation design. Don't worry about the plan being perfect. It's far more important to do something, than to wait until every last detail has been tested.

Work hard to include some interviews in your evaluation methods. Questionnaires don't capture "the story," and the story is usually the most powerful depiction of the benefits of your services.

Don't interview just the successes. You'll learn a great deal about the program by understanding its failures, dropouts, etc.

Don't throw away evaluation results once a report has been generated. Results don't take up much room, and they can provide precious information later when trying to understand changes in the program.

Chapter 13
Lifelong Learning: Don't Ever Stop

When I graduated from the City College of New York in May 1990, my only intention was to work as a chemical engineer. I even completed a Master's degree in engineering management while working at Union Carbide six years later. But God had different plans and I went from engineering management to nonprofit management to community philanthropy.

After about five years in nonprofit management at KISRA, I felt the need to add more tools to my toolbox. An internet search led me to the community economic development program at Southern New Hampshire University (SNHU) in Manchester, New Hampshire. The program was designed for people like me, practitioners who could not quit working full-time while working on their Master's degree.

The School of Community Economic Development at Southern New Hampshire University advocated community development as a strategy for addressing economic problems in communities and societies faced with changing business, social and personal needs. Such development calls for social and economic activities and programs that promote total community benefit rather than individual financial gain. Southern New Hampshire University's School of Community Economic Development was a pioneer in the field when it began offering academic programs in 1982.

We attended classes in-person Fridays through Sundays for the Master's program, while Doctoral program weekends were Thursdays through Mondays. I logged thousands of frequent flyer miles and hotel points during my SNHU days. I'm grateful to the KISRA Board for supporting me in acquiring my Master's degree in 2007 and my Doctorate in 2010 from SNHU. Both degrees were in community economic development (CED).

Designed for the North American practitioner, the Master of Science in National Community Economic Development (NCED) was an applied, 20-month weekend program that offered a unique opportunity for individuals seeking an advanced degree in CED while continuing to work. Classes met for one full weekend each month, usually Friday, Saturday and Sunday, over four semesters (no summer term). An orientation at the beginning of the program and some elective classes were conducted weekdays on class weekend, and a required two-day session takes place in May of the first year. Each student in the program designed a project for implementation in his or her home community. This project was carried on throughout the program's four terms. Students met with project focus groups during class weekends for input, feedback and support, and stayed in contact in between class weekends through Internet discussion groups.

My SNHU education was empowering. It helped me to build my capacity to lead the work we were doing at KISRA. The memorable courses include the following:
- Business Development
- Community Economic Development Theory

- Community Organizing and Community Economic Development
- Evaluation
- Financial Management
- Financing Community Economic Development
- Managerial Accounting
- Microenterprise Development
- Negotiation Strategies
- Nonprofit Management
- Organizational Analysis
- Organizational Management for Community Organizations
- Process Design
- Project Design in Community Economic Development
- Project Evaluation in Community Economic Development
- Project Management in Community Economic Development
- Project Planning in Community Economic Development
- Qualitative Research Methods
- Research Design
- Research Methods
- Research Methods
- Social Inequality
- Social Theory
- Survey Research
- Survey Research Methods
- Theory, Policy and Practice
- Urban Development Theory

After returning from class weekends, I remember immediately implementing the concepts I just learned at work. I was able to finally learn and develop an affinity for logical models as taught by Dr. Jolan Rivera. I found logic models to be a useful tool to guide the design and evaluation of a variety of projects. See more about logic models in Chapter 12.

Unfortunately, the CED program at SNHU no longer exists in this format. The program was dissolved, and the courses were incorporated into the business school. Several of the faculty I knew in the program are now at the University of New Hampshire's Carsey School of Public Policy.

Continuous improvement is a personal core value. So, while at KISRA I also completed two executive education programs at Harvard University and another at University of Oxford. Women and Power and Performance Measurement for Effective Management of Nonprofit Organizations were the Harvard programs along with the Oxford Impact Investing Programme at the Said Business School, University of Oxford.

Women and Power enabled me to:
- Gain new skills and frameworks for analyzing political and strategic management issues
- Examine recent research on women and leadership and its application in the workplace
- Strengthen my negotiation, coalition-building and communication capabilities
- Connect with women leaders from diverse professional backgrounds and similar levels of career achievement

Performance Measurement for Effective Management of Nonprofit Organizations taught me how to:
- Align mission and strategy through performance measurement
- Generate evidence about an intervention's effectiveness
- Build a culture of performance measurement
- Manage for collective impact

The Impact Investment Programme taught me to:
- Work effectively as an impact investment practitioner
- Develop an effective strategy and plan
- Measure and assess impact

Do not ever get to the point in life where you think you know it all; be a life-long learner. You could even learn from a fool. Always be open to new ideas. Always yearn to know more and to be better. Keep stretching. Never think that because you did something a certain way last year, you will do it the same way this year, because that's just the way you've always done it.... no...no...no. Look objectively at the situation, there is always something that can be improved; something that can be refined.

Furthermore, you should have a personal professional development budget. You have to keep your saw sharpened. You have to keep on the cutting edge in order for you to remain competitive.

For example, look at technology. Technology is constantly changing, at lightning speed at times. There are so many options. So many tools. But we have got to do our best to keep up. I never want to be totally reliant on anyone to show me anything. I want to learn and understand for myself.

We not only have to keep up with technology, but we have to keep current on the issues of the day and the evolving issues in the nonprofit sector. Join a nonprofit association. Read nonprofit publications. Attend conferences. Keep current. Keep in the know about your sector. Never stop learning.

Chapter 14
Strategic Planning: Purpose and Direction

Any and all activities your nonprofit is engaged in should align with an overarching strategic plan. Strategic planning is the glue that holds program operations and sustainability efforts together. Without a strategic direction and long-term desired outcomes, nonprofits find themselves only reacting to day-to-day demands. Strategic plans come in various formats. I have even been a part of a strategic planning process based on a logic model design. In general, strategic planning is an organization's process of defining its purpose and making decisions on allocating its resources accordingly. Critical components of a strategic plan are vision, mission, desired outcomes (or goals and objectives) and an action plan.

There are many great reasons to take time to develop a strategic plan:

- It is a foundational element of a well-functional organization
- It creates guidelines and a vision for the future
- It opens ongoing dialogue regarding best practices and programming
- It engages a broad spectrum of people in assuming

ownership – Board members, staff, volunteers and community partners
- It forms the true foundation of a good fundraising plan – diverse sources, timelines, connections
- It builds a solid foundation for program evaluations and staff performance reviews
- It develops skills in the participants and promotes inclusion and retention
- It enables clear articulation of values, so stakeholders feel connected to the mission

Traditional Steps in Strategic Planning:
1. Identify stakeholders and set a timeline. Stakeholders include Board of directors, staff, volunteers, and key community partners. The timeline includes pre-work, assessments, in person sessions, plan completion and future updates.
2. Assess the current situation within the organization and community. This may include surveys and gathering of secondary data on community indicators.
3. Honestly assess strengths and weaknesses. Strengths are internal, positive attributes of an organization. They are the characteristics that give the organization its competitive advantage. Strengths are those things that are within your control. Weaknesses are negative factors that detract from your strengths. These are things that you might need to improve on to be competitive. Weaknesses are characteristics that an organization needs to overcome in order to improve its performance.

4. Look at the economic, political and demographic environments, they can affect the organization. Consider the impact the COVID-19 pandemic has had on all of our lives.

5. Define broad strategic directions in line with the vision of the organization.

6. Design a way to check in on the plan and evaluate progress. Don't just develop the plan and put it on a shelf. Run with it. Share it broadly.

7. Make the plan operational by attaching timelines, assigning responsibilities and creating a budget.

8. Implement the plan. It should be a living, breathing document.

I recommend retaining a third party to facilitate your strategic planning process and secure funding from a funding partner to pay for it.

SWOT Analysis

Assessing an organization's strengths, weaknesses, opportunities and threats are a common part of strategic planning processes. Strengths and weaknesses are often internal to the organization, while opportunities and threats generally relate to external factors.

Strengths: Questions to Consider
- What are your assets?
- What differentiates you from other organizations providing similar services and products?

- Do you have immensely talented people on your staff?
- Do you have a broad stakeholder base?
- What unique resources do you have?
- Do you have a sustainable competitive advantage?
- Do you have specific areas of expertise?
- Do you have a good story to tell?
- Do you have community champions that tell your story to the masses?
- Do you have a diverse funding base?

Weaknesses: Questions to Consider
- In what areas do you need to improve?
- What necessary expertise/personnel do you currently lack?
- In what areas do other service providers have an edge?
- Are you relying on one funding source too much?
- Do you have adequate cash flow to sustain us?
- Do you have a well of new ideas?
- Do you have an attractive salary and benefits structure to attract and retain the best staff?
- Do you have the appropriate Board members?
- Are you an inclusive organization?
- Are you using current technology?
- Are staff members attending professional development activities?

Opportunities: Questions to Consider
- What external changes present interesting opportunities?
- What trends might impact your industry?
- Is there talent located elsewhere that you might be able to acquire?

- Is a competitor/another service provider failing to adequately service the market?
- Is there an unmet need/want that you can fulfill?

Threats: Questions to Consider

- Is there a better equipped (funding, talent, mobility, etc.) competitor in your market?
- Is there an entity who may not be a competitor today which could possibly become one tomorrow?
- Are your key staff satisfied in their work? Could they be poached by a competitor?
- Is your intellectual property properly secured (trademarks, copyrights, firewalls, data security plans, etc.) against theft & loss (both from internal & external sources)?
- Do you rely on third parties for critical steps in your development process that could possibly derail our delivery schedule?
- What if you are sued?
- Are you relying too heavily on a particular grantor?
- What if a long-term grantor changes their priorities?
- Are your systems secure enough to withstand a cyber-attack?

Now what?

- *Strengths:* How can you leverage them?
- *Weaknesses:* How can you minimize or eliminate them?
- *Opportunities:* How can you capitalize on these while possibly eliminating weaknesses or threats?
- *Threats:* Evaluate opportunities that can address the threats.

Strategic Issues

- What are the major immediate and near-term issues that you must address?
- What are the major obstacles or issues that you face?
- What are the more forward-looking, developmental goals to accomplish over the next few years?

Strategic Goals

- What are the strategic goals to address the identified issues?
- Goals should be SMARTER... **S**pecific, **M**easurable, **A**cceptable to the people working to achieve the goals, **R**ealistic, **T**imely, **E**xtending the capabilities of those working to achieve the goals and **R**ewarding to them.

Action Planning
Who is going to do what and by when? Refer to Appendix K for a Sample Work Plan.

Chapter 15
Financial Management Essentials

The eagle eye is among the sharpest in the animal kingdom, with an eyesight estimated at 4 to 8 times stronger than the average human. This is the level of intensity you should focus on your finances.

Accurate record keeping and reporting are mandatory for non-profits as the US government imposes strict reporting regulations and fiduciary compliance rules. It is important to establish a robust financial management system to reduce the likelihood of fraudulent activities. Fraud can result in financial and credibility losses to an organization. Your system should be capable of easily tracking expenses by grants and generating reports to facilitate reporting needed by grantors.

Grantors want to ensure that grantees use their grants as intended in the grant applications that are approved, to achieve the desired community impact. They rely on independent auditors to assess grantees records and processes. When I was at KISRA, one federal grantor required us to submit a notarized Affidavit of Standards for Financial Management Systems. We had to attest to the following:

Our financial management systems conform to the financial accountability standards set forth in 24 CFR 84.21 (b) and 85.20, by providing for and incorporating the following:

a. Accurate, current and complete disclosure of the financial results of each federally-sponsored project.

b. Records which identify the source and application of funds for federally-sponsored activities. These records contain information pertaining to Federal awards, authorizations, obligations, unobligated balances, assets, outlays, income and interest.

c. Control over and accountability for all funds, property and other assets. Adequate safeguards of all such assets shall be adopted to assure that they are used solely for authorized purposes.

d. Comparison of outlays with budget amounts for each award.

e. Written procedures to minimize the time elapsing between the receipt of funds and the issuance or redemption of checks for program purposes by the recipient.

f. Written procedures for determining the reasonableness, allocability and allowability of costs in accordance with the provisions of Federal cost principles [Circular A-122] and the terms and conditions of the award.

g. Accounting records, including cost-accounting records, that are supported by source documentation.

The federal guidelines are the most stringent, but if you set up your process and systems to meet them, then you will meet other grantors' requirements.

§ 85.20 Standards for financial management systems.

(1) **Financial reporting**. Accurate, current and complete disclosure of the financial results of financially assisted activities must be made in accordance with the financial reporting requirements of the grant or subgrant.

(2) **Accounting records.** Grantees and subgrantees must maintain records which adequately identify the source and application of funds provided for financially-assisted activities. These records must contain information pertaining to grant or subgrant awards and authorizations, obligations, unobligated balances, assets, liabilities, outlays or expenditures and income.

(3) **Internal control.** Effective control and accountability must be maintained for all grant and subgrant cash, real and personal property, and other assets. Grantees and subgrantees must adequately safeguard all such property and must assure that it is used solely for authorized purposes.

(4) **Budget control.** Actual expenditures or outlays must be compared with budgeted amounts for each grant or subgrant. Financial information must be related to performance or productivity data, including the development of unit cost information whenever appropriate or specifically required in the grant or subgrant agreement. If unit cost data are required, estimates based on available documentation will be accepted whenever possible.

(5) **Allowable cost.** Applicable OMB cost principles, agency program regulations, and the terms of grant and subgrant agreements will be followed in determining the reasonableness, allowability and allocability of costs.

(6) **Source documentation.** Accounting records must be supported by such source documentation as cancelled checks, paid bills, payrolls, time and attendance records, contract and subgrant award documents, etc.

(7) **Cash management.** Procedures for minimizing the time elapsing between the transfer of funds from the U.S. Treasury and disbursement by grantees and subgrantees must be followed whenever advance payment procedures are used. Grantees must establish reasonable procedures to ensure the receipt of reports on subgrantees' cash balances and cash disbursements in sufficient time to enable them to prepare complete and accurate cash transactions reports to the awarding agency. When advances are made by letter-of-credit or electronic transfer of funds methods, the grantee must make drawdowns as close as possible to the time of making disbursements. Grantees must monitor cash drawdowns by their 8 24 CFR PART 85 subgrantees to assure that they conform substantially to the same standards of timing and amount as apply to advances to the grantees.

Considerations

1) **Internal controls:** Does your organization have a written set of policies and procedures that define staff qualifications and duties, lines of authority, separation of functions and access to assets and sensitive documents? Does your organization have written accounting procedures for approving and recording transactions? Are financial records periodically compared to actual assets and liabilities to check for completeness and accuracy?

2) **Accounting records:** Does your organization maintain an adequate financial accounting system, the basic elements of which should include: (a) a chart of accounts, (b) a general ledger, (c) a cash receipts journal, (d) a cash disbursements journal, (e) a payroll journal, (f) payable and receivable ledgers and (g) job cost journals (if involved in construction)? Does your accounting system provide reliable, complete and up-to-date information about sources and uses of all funds? Are "trial balances" performed on a regular basis (at least quarterly)?

3) **Allowable costs:** Does your organization have a clearly defined set of standards and procedures for determining the reasonableness, allowability and allocability of costs incurred that's consistent with the basic Federal rules (OMB Circulars A-87 or A-122)?

4) **Source documentation:** Does your organization maintain up-to-date files of original source documentation (receipts, invoices, canceled checks, etc.) for all of your financial transactions?

5) **Budget controls:** Does your organization maintain an up-to-date (approved) budget for all funded activities, and perform a comparison of that budget with actual expenditures for each budget category? Does your organization regularly compare progress toward the achievement of goals with the rate of expenditure of program funds?

6) **Cash management:** Does your organization have a regular procedure for accurately projecting the cash needs of the

organization that will serve to minimize the time between the receipt of funds from the grantee and their actual disbursement?

7) **Financial reporting:** Is your organization able to provide accurate, current and complete disclosure of the financial results of each Federally-sponsored project or program in accordance with the reporting requirements of the grantee and HUD?

8) **Audits:** When was your last Independent Public Accountant (IPA) audit and what were the results? Does your organization have a copy of the management letter?

Internal controls are critical. These controls are the mechanisms, rules and procedures implemented by an organization to ensure financial and accounting information integrity, promote accountability and prevent fraud.

Kelly Shafer, a Certified Public Accountant with Suttle and Stalnaker, recommends the following ways an organization can strengthen internal controls:
- Segregate duties - don't have the same person open the mail, prepare deposits, take the deposit to the bank, and record the transaction
- Only allow employees access to areas they need to perform their job
- An employee who can sign checks should not also have exclusive access to the check stock
- Require dual signatures on checks
- Have monetary authorization limits
- Avoid signature stamps

- Monthly bank statements should be mailed directly to a Board member for review or provide access to online banking
- Review credit card charges and reconcile the monthly statement
- If using electronic approvals, keep a paper trail (emails)
- Cross-train employees
- Require annual vacations
- Conduct background checks
- Have annual audit/review
- Establish a fraud tip line

Remember, internal controls protect an organization as well as its employees.

To facilitate your financial recordkeeping, I recommend utilizing a software system like QuickBooks. QuickBooks is affordable and accessible. Remember TechSoup, a source for nonprofits to purchase software and hardware at deep discounts.

Build a reserve fund

Some community-based nonprofits experience funding fluctuations from time to time, disrupting their operations. Building a reserve fund that can be accessed during these uncertain times is vital to sustainability. A reserve of at least six months of the organization's annual operating budget is ideal.

Building this reserve will not be easy for many, but it is definitely worth the effort to tuck away as much as you can to sustain your organization. You can establish your fund at a local community foundation or other financial institution that offers a generous rate of return.

Chapter 16

Role Models and Mentors: We All Need Them

Winston and Muline Mickle, my parents, are my role models. They are my best examples of tenacity, generosity and philanthropy.

I watched them study to advance their careers and I saw them work hard to afford a modest lifestyle for us while in Guyana and after we immigrated to Brooklyn. My mom was a lecturer at the Teachers Training College when she left Guyana, and my dad was the Chief Financial Officer at the General Post Office. They restarted their careers when we immigrated. When they moved to Brooklyn, my mom was happy at her first job at a childcare center, while my dad got dressed every morning and waited for that telephone call to instruct him where show up for a temporary office position. They eventually rose through the ranks to re-establish careers to match their level of education.

Our first five years were spent living in my aunt Norma's small basement, while they worked hard, saved and paid their taxes. By our fifth year they had saved up enough money to purchase a house. Today that house is paid off as they enjoy their retirement.

They also are very generous and liberally support family members in need in the US and Guyana. I distinctly remember when my mom spontaneously passed the hat during our first family reunion gathering, for us to bless my cousin, a pastor, who had delivered the sermonette for the closing gathering. This is just the type of person she is.

While in Guyana, extended family members were always living with us. My parents often send money home to Guyana for family members and support educational programs there as well. They even financially support extended family in the US when they are in need. I am not sure how they have been able to afford the gifts, but they have been very frugal with their resources. For example, my mom had no loyalty to food brands. The house was stocked with whatever was on sale that week. We ate at home, except for the occasional Chinese takeout on Friday evenings. She was cost conscious about everything. She preferred to buy a tub of ice cream than go out to the ice cream shop for cones.

Pastor Emanuel Alphonso Heyliger is my spiritual father and mentor. I had the honor of being the speaker at his 42nd pastor's anniversary celebration at Ferguson Memorial Baptist Church in June 2022. "Lessons Learned from a Spiritual Father" was the title of my message. Here are the lessons that I shared.

Lesson 1: Sing even when no one thinks you should

"Make a joyful noise unto God," is written in several Psalms. Pastor takes this scripture to heart. He loves to praise the Lord, in season and out of season, in his own key. And don't even try to quench his spirit, because it just makes him sing even louder and dance even more. His boldness in praising God has liberated my praise because I too was not blessed with a good singing voice. He has taught me that regardless of what I am going through; regardless of if I feel like it; regardless of what others may say or others may think, all praise belongs to God.

Pastor reminds me that I have so many reasons to praise God. God has kept me these 50 plus years. I have great health and strength. When people my age and younger are transitioning, I am so blessed to be standing strong. God provides for me. He uses me in his service. He orchestrates all aspects of my life.

> Psalms 34:1 - I will bless the LORD at all times: his praise shall continually be in my mouth.

When you are active in ministry, sometimes you will be so discouraged that you wouldn't want to come to church. Sometimes you will get so discouraged that if you make it to church, you just want to sit there all lethargic, regardless of what the worship leader, praise team, choir or pastor is doing. Trust me it will happen! But remember the words of the psalmist when he said, "I will bless the lord at all times." All times means that there will be good times and bad times; happy times and sad times; fruitful times and barren times; times of growth and times of decay. But you know what, we have to praise God through it all if we are going to endure in ministry. And Pastor Heyliger lives this, he has endured in ministry for 42 years.

Lesson 2: Two people can't act the fool at the same time

Pastor has taught me how to resolve conflicts by remembering that two people can't act the fool at the same time.

Not so much now, but in my early years at FMBC, I sat through many meetings where Pastor was attacked by members. Members who were downright nasty. I was often shocked. I expected church to be Utopia, where everyone got along, and everything was hunky-dory. Boy was I wrong. I am amazed at what pastors put up with, especially when they have been at their posts for decades.

Instead of striking back, he would sit there and let them get whatever they needed off their chests and then proceed to get the meeting back on track. He never went at the person in public. I learned people skills and conflict resolution from Pastor Heyliger.

Biblical conflict resolution is outlined in Matthew 18:15-18

> Moreover, if thy brother shall trespass against thee, go and tell him his fault between thee and him alone: if he shall hear thee, thou hast gained thy brother.

> But if he will not hear thee, then take with thee one or two more, that in the mouth of two or three witnesses every word may be established.

> And if he shall neglect to hear them, tell it unto the church: but if he neglect to hear the church, let him be unto thee as a heathen man and a publican.

Verily I say unto you, Whatsoever ye shall bind on earth shall be bound in heaven: and whatsoever ye shall loose on earth shall be loosed in heaven.

If someone is acting the fool and attacking you in public, nothing good will come out of you going right back at them in public. Follow the Biblical conflict resolution steps. Talk to them one-on-one because two people can't act the fool at the same time.

Lesson 3: Always find refuge in God

The psalmist wrote that God is our refuge and strength, A *very present help* in trouble. I have seen Pastor Heyliger live out this scripture time and time again.

Pastor has experienced rough times: in his personal life, with his family, in his vocational life at the church and in his health, but he always finds refuge in God. In the worst of times, he has stuck to what he knows best; proclaiming what thus said the Lord. Praying for others. Reading and studying the word of God and numerous Biblical books.

I remember the time when as a baby, his granddaughter Emani accidently ingested someone else's medication. As you could imagine, he was distraught, shaken to the core. Nevertheless, he came to church; he preached; he prayed at the altar; then headed back to the hospital..

From watching him I know to keep calm when trials come. I know to take my challenges to God and let him fight my battles.

And do you know what, everything does work together for good. God still amazes me! Being a Christian or even a Pastor doesn't mean that you will be immune from the vicissitudes of life. Sometimes I believe the devil brings out his whole arsenal against us. But in spite of it all, we can find refuge in God.

Lesson 4: Grant grace liberally

> And he said unto me, "My *grace* is sufficient for thee: for my strength is made perfect in weakness. Most gladly therefore will I rather glory in my infirmities, that the power of Christ may rest upon me." (II Corinthians 12:9)

Grace is God's unmerited favor. Grace is all the chances God gives us to get our act together.

I see this in Pastor, he grants grace liberally. He doesn't hold grudges. I used to be irritated when I would see him give people chance after chance, even when they disappointed him. I was irritated because I didn't fully grasp the concept of grace. Grace is being quick to forgive others, just like God forgives us over and over and over again. We are to forgive those who have wronged us. We have to forgive those who are not true to their word. Everyone needs a chance to get it right. God is still working on us all. We are still being sanctified.

God's grace is the spontaneous, unmerited gift of the divine favor in the salvation of sinners and the divine influence operating in individuals for their regeneration and sanctification.

"So let us therefore come boldly unto the throne of grace,

that we may obtain mercy and find grace to help in time of need." (Hebrews 4:16.)

Pastor emulates God's grace and so should we.

Lesson 5: We need a vision to see beyond our current circumstances

Habakkuk 2:1-3 (KJV) reads, "I will stand upon my watch, and set me upon the tower, and will watch to see what he will say unto me, and what I shall answer when I am reproved. And the LORD answered me, and said, Write the vision, and make *it* plain upon tables, that he may run that readeth it. For the vision *is* yet for an appointed time, but at the end it shall speak, and not lie: though it tarry, wait for it; because it will surely come, it will not tarry."

Pastor is a visionary. He has unusual foresight and imagination that intersects with a strong faith in God. I wasn't here when this church was built, but I heard stories. He had few supporters initially, but he kept pressing forward and eventually the people caught the vision. We have long since paid off this church and are operating with no debt at all. What a blessing!

Pastor taught me to write the vision, run with the vision, tarry for the vision and the vision will speak. This was our mantra in church for several years. And I have used it in other areas of my life. This passage gives me hope for the future. It gives me hope as I tarry.

When my hope quotient gets low, I have to remind myself to whom I have committed my life to serving. I remind myself that I serve a God who took five loaves and two fishes and fed thousands. I remind myself that I serve a God who made the deaf to hear, the lame to walk, and the blind to see. I remind myself that I serve a God who is able to do exceeding, abundantly above all that I may ask or think. Even though I may not be able to think or imagine it, he is still able to do it. Even though I can't conceive it he is still able to do it.

Focusing on a vision leaves little room for complaining.
Focusing on a vision leaves little room for knit-picking.
Focusing on a vision leaves little room back-biting, jealousy and strife.
Focusing on a vision leaves little room for trifling people who aren't about anything.

Without a vision we will surely perish.

Lesson 6: Everyone is fallible
All have sinned and come short of the glory of God (Romans 3:23).

Let me be clear, the fact that I am sharing lessons learned from my spiritual father does not mean I believe that Pastor is perfect. Not at all. He has his flaws. So, do I. So do you. Remember, only Jesus is perfect.

What Pastor Heyliger is, is a man after God's own heart. He loves the Lord with all his soul and with all his might. He has that great faith, and he is not intimidated by any mountain. He taught me that it's better for the mountain to be rough so that you can find places to hang on as you climb, and it makes sense. Pastor has more faith than anyone I have ever known. Sometimes I just have to look at him and shake my head, because I don't always see it. But he is a man after God's own heart.

Although I am flawed, I am striving every day to be a woman after God's own heart just as Pastor exemplifies.

Lesson 7: Ministry is meeting needs

Pastor taught me the best definition of ministry :

> Ministry is meeting needs
> Ministry is serving God through your service to mankind
> Ministry is not just inside the church walls; it is in the community
> Ministry is not getting involved so that you can be seen, it includes a lot of work behind the scenes and can be very lonely
> Ministry is not being stuck up under the Pastor

What I noticed in my early years is that the people who get involved in ministry just to be seen or to be up under the pastor, never last. They are hot and heavy one minute and the next minute they are nowhere to be seen!

The scripture that comes to mind for this particular lesson is Luke 4:18-19.

> The Spirit of the Lord is upon me, because He hath anointed me to preach the gospel to the poor; He hath sent me to heal the brokenhearted, to preach deliverance

to the captives, And recovering of sight to the blind, To set at liberty them that are bruised, To preach the acceptable year of the Lord.

We are anointed to do ministry. I am so grateful that Pastor inspired me to engage in ministry. Like Paul stirred up gifts in Timothy, Pastor Heyliger stirred up gifts in me I never knew that I had which has been life transforming for me. He stirred up my gifts and trusted me with the opportunity to use them in this church and in the community through KISRA.

I had the opportunity of a lifetime to pursue my passion. The opportunity to engage in work that set my soul on fire, which led to my current career as a philanthropy leader.

I remember being so nervous to tell Pastor that I had received the job offer from the Greater Kanawha Valley Foundation. When I finally did, he wasn't mad. He was happy for me; happy that others saw my value.

Every leader can benefit from role models and mentors.

Chapter 17
Prioritize Self-Care: Operate at Your Peak

Many of my KISRA years are now a blur. All I did was work. After my marriage ended, I buried myself in work. Working evenings and weekends were the norm. I was always the last person to leave the office in the evenings. I struggled with my weight and realized I needed to take better care of myself, but I always came last.

I suffered with uterine fibroids for years. The heavy bleeding left me anemic. It wasn't until 2008 that I finally decided to do something about it. Birth control pills were effective in controlling the bleeding for years and I was managing. But then they stopped working, and it seemed like I was forever on my period. I remember I was on Capitol Hill for a visit with our congressional delegation along with two male board members. I was so embarrassed about my frequent trips to the restroom. The fibroids were affecting my quality of life and I had to do something about it.

I scheduled an appointment at Ruby Memorial Hospital in Morgantown to consult with a doctor about the uterine artery embolization procedure. It so happened that the day after,

I mentioned to our insurance agent at the time about what I considering. She mentioned a less invasive procedure that Charleson-based Dr. David Patton performed. A laparoscopic supracervical hysterectomy was perfect for me. It is a minimally invasive procedure in which a woman's uterus is removed using a technique that involves several small abdominal incisions. The recovery time was about one week. This was ideal because I was running KISRA and working on my doctorate at the time.

As we live through these COVID years, the need for self-care has become increasingly important. Self-care is the practice of taking an active role in protecting one's well-being and happiness, especially during periods of stress. Self-care is not selfish. Self-care is not indulgent. Self-care is necessary for us to cope in the midst of chaos.

There is nothing great about being too busy to rest and take care of your health. You are only setting yourself up for burn out, mental illness and broken relationships. Even Jesus rested and advised others to rest especially after big events and in preparation for them. Are you resting?

Sleep is the balm that soothes and restores after a long day. Sleep is largely driven by the body's internal clock, which takes cues from external elements such as sunlight and temperature. The body's natural sleep-and-wake cycle is reasonably attuned to a 24-hour period.

Changes in the sleep cycle are disruptive to the functioning of many body systems. Learning, memory, stamina, general health and mood are all affected by sleep duration and quality. Potential consequences of consistently poor sleep include obesity, cardiovascular disease and diabetes. Sleep deprivation can also affect judgement and mental acuity.

Sleep needs differ from person to person and across different age groups. One person may need eight full hours, while another can function with less sleep. But we all need to sleep we all need that rest.

Resting may be hard for many of us to accept. Our modern society moves at a blinding speed, and we're constantly told to work longer, achieve higher, and contribute more often. Even on the weekends, our schedules overflow with tasks like doing laundry, cleaning the house, fixing the car or shuffling the kids off to sports practice. We have effectively forgotten how to rest.

True relaxation is necessary for a healthy mind. We need to take breaks! Spend some time reading a fun book, do a puzzle, take a nap, get a pedicure or grab a massage. Resting is an effective self-care practice.

Withdrawing and practicing mindfulness are also a part of self-care. It's alright to withdraw. It's okay to need alone time. Amidst all the demands of life, all of the appointments to keep, the meetings/parties to host, the networking events to attend, the dinners to cook, the children to raise, the reports to complete, the paychecks to earn, the friends to comfort or celebrate with, we sometimes need to withdraw.

This might be a weekend away by yourself. This might be an hour on a weekend where you retreat to a comfy chair with a book or some music and lock the door behind you. Your family and friends will last for that long without you. And if you make it a habit, they will begin to understand and to embrace it.

Practicing mindfulness can be as simple as a 3- to 5-minute meditation or prayer each morning. **Mindfulness** meditation early in the day can lower levels of the stress hormone cortisol (which fuels the fight-or-flight instinct) when it is most elevated. Mindfulness quiets down those areas of the brain that are overly active and constantly firing over time.

Mindfulness is really about being in the moment, observing what's coming at you from the outside and what's coming up inside—taking it in and observing, and not reacting to it. With extended practice, you can begin to let go of what's coming at you. There are even free mindfulness apps on your phone that you can utilize.

Chapter 18
Gratitude and Hope: Key Attributes for Your Endurance

Gratitude is an important characteristic of leadership and success. Charles Patton, Former Appalachian Power, Chief Operations Officer

Expressing gratitude is one of the most effective ways to become not only a better leader but also a better person. Gratitude is the quality of being thankful; readiness to show appreciation for and to return kindness. Gratitude is a practice, not a character trait. As leaders we should cultivate gratitude because it breeds engagement and more positive interactions. What's more, gratitude helps you acknowledge your accomplishments.

Thankfulness encourages you to focus on your successes. You will not be consumed by the success or failures of your competitors, and you'll be making the world better for those around you. Gratitude, while allowing you to embrace your accomplishments, also keeps your ego in check. That's because appreciation will enable you to realize that without assistance from others, you wouldn't be as successful. Maybe it's because you have a spouse who was your primary source of support and inspiration. A business partner provided you with the finances to launch your business. Or, thanks to their hard work and dedication, your business idea has become a reality because of your employees. Additionally, when we're thankful and optimistic, others gravitate towards us. Being approachable and encouraging is critical when networking and attracting top talent.

To practice gratitude on a daily basis, you can start by blocking out a specific time on your calendar, to make it a priority, and even keeping a journal. Complimenting your team members daily is also key. Give them the opportunity to voice their opinions and share their ideas, they will feel more valued. By doing so, you are letting them know that you want them involved in big decisions and successes. You can also practice gratitude by creating positive work culture. We celebrate birthdays. Have potluck lunches or go out to lunch periodically. We also attend fun community events together. Fostering a positive work culture will make your team more productive, happy, creative and collaborative.

A high hope quotient will help you to endure

"We must accept finite disappointment, but never lose infinite hope." Martin Luther King, Jr. spoke these words in a Washington, D.C. address in February 1968, just two months before he was assassinated in Memphis. In his personal and public life, he endured many disappointments. Dr. King encouraged that we accept those challenges even as we hold onto the hope that makes his message so relevant. A disappointment or setback can put any of us in danger of giving up on our goals, hopes and dreams, whether for ourselves or for the world. Accepting that setback is simply part of the road toward what he famously called "the promised land" frees us to process our

failures in a larger context of progress, connection and above all, hope. I have decided to make hope my superpower!

Some wise person said that we can live about 40 days without food. We can live about three days without water. We can live about eight minutes without air. But we can't live a single second without hope.

You see...

The greatest gift leaders can give their team member is hope.

The greatest gift parents can give their children is hope.

The greatest gift teachers can give their students is hope.

The greatest gift coaches can give their athletes is hope.

The greatest gift we can give our friends is hope.

Folks who have researched the subject of hope, have found that the presence of hope and confidence is impactful in a number of ways:

- We have more satisfying relationships
- We are more productive
- We are less affected by stress
- We are more successful
- We feel more satisfied
- We are more compassionate
- We are more willing to help people in need
- We are physically healthier
- We hold ourselves to higher ethical and moral standards
- We are more likely to assume leadership

Chapter 19
Sustainability:
It's More than Money

Sustainability capacity is the ability to maintain an initiative and its benefits over time. It is meeting the needs of the present without compromising the ability of future generations to meet their own needs.

Nonprofit leaders should always keep sustainability at the forefront of their minds. It is important to note that sustainability is more than just funding. While at KISRA I learned about the Sustainability Framework from the Brown School of Social Work at Washington University in St. Louis.

To improve capacity for sustainability, they encourage strengthening structures and processes that exist within your program to ensure you can strategically leverage resources to weather the changes and challenges that come your way. The Sustainability Framework has eight key domains that can influence a program's capacity for sustainability. They are:

- Environmental support
- Funding stability
- Partnerships

- Organizational capacity
- Program evaluation
- Program adaptation
- Communications
- Strategic planning

Environmental support is having a supportive internal and external climate for your program. No matter the level at which your program operates, the overall economic and political climate will affect your ability to get things done. Whether or not decision makers support your cause, they deserve your attention. Work to get people of influence on your side, both within and outside of your organization. Often these decision makers control the money, and if you want some for your program, you will need them to know and like your program. In addition, champions can get policies passed that benefit your target population and help achieve your program goals.

Funding stability is establishing a consistent financial base for your program. Planning for stable funding should be a strategic process that addresses the long-term needs of your program and adjusts to changing trends in economic and political cycles. Funding highs and lows put stress on programs and make it difficult to provide consistent quality services. Programs that rely on a single funding source, rather than multiple sources, are more vulnerable when funding cuts occur. For all these reasons, it's important to build a stable and diverse funding base.

Partnerships is about cultivating connections between your program and its stakeholders. Partners play an important role in sustainability in several ways: connecting you to greater resources or expertise, providing services if your program has to cut back and advocating on behalf of your cause. Partners can also help rally the community around your program and its goals. They can range from business leaders and media representatives to organizations addressing similar issues and community members. When your program is threatened either politically or financially, your partners can be some of your greatest champions. Building awareness and capacity for sustainability requires a strategic approach and partnerships across sectors, including alliances between private and public organizations.

Organizational capacity is having the internal support and resources needed to effectively manage your program. Organizational capacity encompasses a wide range of capabilities, knowledge and resources. For example, having enough staff and strong leadership can make a big difference in accomplishing your program goals. Cultivating and strengthening your program's internal support can also increase your program's likelihood of long-term success.

Program evaluation is assessing your program to inform planning and document results. Evaluation helps keep your program on track with its goals and outcomes. If evaluation data shows that an activity or strategy isn't working, you can correct your program's course to become more effective.
Moreover, collecting data about your program's successes and impact is a powerful tool for gaining support and funding. If your evaluation data shows that your program is making an important (or irreplaceable) impact, you can make a strong case

for why your program needs to continue. Even in times of decreased funding, evaluation and monitoring data are key for the pursuit of new funding sources.

Program adaptation is taking actions that adapt your program to ensure its ongoing effectiveness. Circumstances change and sometimes your program needs to as well. The goal is not necessarily to sustain all of a program's components over time, but rather to sustain the most effective components and their benefits to your target group. This requires flexibility, adaptation to changing conditions and quality improvement within your program. By using your evaluation data and current evidence-base, you can ensure that your program effectively uses resources and continues having an impact.

Communications is about strategic communication with stakeholders and the public about your program. People need to know what your program does and why it's important. Communicating externally about your program's effectiveness helps the program gain greater visibility and builds support from stakeholders. Internally, evidence that a program works builds staff buy-in and support from organizational leaders. The more people know and care about your program and mission, the more likely they are to support your efforts to continue providing services in the long term.

Strategic planning is using processes that guide your program's directions, goals and strategies. Strategic planning is the glue that holds sustainability efforts together. Without a strategic direction and long-term goals, programs find themselves only reacting to day-to-day demands. Strategic planning combines elements of all of the sustainability domains into an outcome-oriented plan. Planning also ensures that the program is well aligned with the larger external and organizational environment.

I cover a number of these domains in different chapters of this book. However, I recommend going to the website sustaintool. org for additional resources.

Chapter 20
My New Season

There is a season for everything, and a time for every event under heaven: Ecclesiastes 3:1

On December 9, 2015, I resigned as CEO of the Kanawha Institute for Social Research & Action, Inc. (KISRA). As I wrote in my resignation letter, September 2015 marked the beginning of the eighteenth year of KISRA serving the citizens of West Virginia. It was my honor to nurture the organization through its period of development from infancy to adulthood. However, God in his infinite wisdom, had orchestrated a new season in my life and consequently, in the life of KISRA.

On Monday, February 8, 2016, I began my new season as the President and CEO of The Greater Kanawha Valley Foundation (TGKVF). I did not initially pursue this position, as I was not in the market for new employment. In fact, TGKVF's recruiter reached out to me several months prior to assess my interest in the position, because as he stated, "your name keeps coming up." After prayerful consideration, I decided to submit to the interview process, as I believed this could be the perfect next phase in my career. As God would have it, I was the candidate the search committee recommended to the Foundation Board of directors.

I thank the KISRA Board of directors for the opportunity to pursue my passion and to stir up the gifts that the creator deposited within me. It was an epic journey. My last day with KISRA was Friday, February 5, 2016.

I am enjoying my career with TGKVF. It is a more visible position than my KISRA position as the Foundation is a revered community institution located in downtown Charleston, the capital city. The KISRA headquarters is in Dunbar. I am honored to be the 4th President and CEO in the history of the foundation and the first Black person in this position of leadership. In fact, I do not know of another Black Foundation president in Central Appalachia.

As the President and CEO, I report to the Board of Trustees, and I am responsible for the overall day-to-day leadership of the Foundation. Priorities of this position focus on delivering the highest quality donor services while safeguarding the financial sustainability of the organization through prudent business practices. I provide leadership in executing an innovative strategic plan; in collaborating with other leaders and decision-makers in the broader community; in providing the vision to address future challenges and opportunities in the community; in fostering a developmental organizational climate that builds staff competencies and supports professional growth and development; and by representing the Foundation as its key spokesperson and representative in the community.

My essential functions and responsibilities:

- Develop, present and manages the implementation of strategic plans to advance the Foundation's interests.

- Oversee the development and marketing activities of the Foundation, including developing and overseeing a comprehensive program of donor acknowledgment and recognition.

- Maintain a high level of community involvement to develop a network of donor prospects and relationships with local financial advisors and to seek opportunities for the Foundation to fulfill its mission through grantmaking and program management.

- Build and maintain ties with a variety of constituencies throughout the community who will help the Foundation in its endeavors and manage prospect relationships, including identification, cultivation and solicitation of top-level prospects.

- Serve as consultant on all Board Committees including standing and ad hoc committees or task forces; facilitate the preparation of information and material needed by each committee; and coordinate the work of committees so as to avoid overlaps or gaps in progress toward accomplishment of goals. Serve as primary staff support for the Advisory Committee, Executive Committee and Nominating Committee.

- Oversee the management system to provide affiliate services.

- Work directly with the Chairman of the Board of Trustees in implementing Board decisions, coordinating work of Board Committees, developing goals and long-range planning and reviewing progress toward goals.

- Employ and supervise staff and oversee a continuous process of staff development.

- Assist the Chairman of the Board in planning and preparing Board Agendas; facilitate the preparation of Board Books, and attend Board meetings in ex- official capacity, serving as a consultant.

- Establish organizational plans, policies and procedures for the organization. Design the annual budget and operating structure of the Foundation and organize and assign major accountabilities and functions as needed.

- Keep the Board informed of activities, problems, and/or progress between Board meetings; maintain service records of Board members and arrange training as needed to enhance the progress toward reaching the goals of the Foundation and work to ensure that each Board member is recognized and shown appreciation for his/her work on behalf of the Foundation.

- Serve as a spokesperson to advance the cause of private philanthropy in the community. Oversee publicity and public relations activities, seeking opportunities for public speaking and developing positive relationships with local and area media.

- Identify community issues and recommend ways in which the Foundation can address those issues.

- Represent the Foundation along with other grant makers in planning community wide initiatives and develop and maintain ties with national organizations in the field of philanthropy.

As I am finishing up this book, the Foundation is wrapping up its 60th anniversary year. As we reflect on our history, I believe it is important to note that volunteers handled the operations, grantmaking and administration of the Foundation in the early years. The late Stanley Loewenstein volunteered as the inaugural executive director from 1980 to 1986. He was followed by Betsy VonBlond. My predecessor, Becky Ceperley, was appointed in 1999. Becky has been the longest serving Foundation leader in the 60-year history. I thank Becky for establishing the infrastructure of the organization. I appreciate her for leaving a solid foundation for me to build upon when I began my tenure in 2016.

TGKVF is the largest community foundation in central Appalachia, a philanthropy leader in the region. The word "philanthropy" means love of humankind. Our community is blessed by the many people who express a love for humankind through their giving. The Foundation is a philanthropic leader that helps donors, nonprofits and other collaborative partners strengthen our community so all of the people and places we serve have the opportunity to thrive.

We have come a long way from our first gift in 1962. It was a gift of $100 from members of the Charleston Municipal Planning Commission in memory of Robert S. Spilman, III. We started our discretionary grantmaking program in 1965 with a grant of

$1,000 to Morris Harvey College (now University of Charleston) to support students in the nursing program. Fast forwarding 60 years, we received $3.8 million in contributions and distributed $13.1 million in grants and scholarships in 2021. We have distributed over $183 million in grants over the last 60 years. At the end of 2021, the Foundation had $329 million in assets under management, distributed among 555 individual funds.

TGKVF accomplishments under my watch as of December 2022 include the following:

- The assets under management and number of funds have grown
- Technology upgrades have included new computer systems and an efficient local computer network
- We have a new, visible, modern office
- Staff growth – we are now a 14-member team that used to be 9 when I arrived
- All staff are more visible in the local and philanthropy communities
- Each staff member has an annual professional development budget
- We have a modern website
- All promotional materials, like newsletters and scholarship brochures, are professionally designed
- We have a more significant social media presence on four different platforms
- We have a podcast – Philanthropy & Friends
- We measure community level indicators on a regular basis
- Grantee reporting is now online

- There is now systematic capacity building/organizational strengthening support for grantee partners in a leadership institute and funding for emerging nonprofits
- We have a more diverse operations team – race and gender
- We retained an independent grantee perception analysis to inform our strategic plan
- We simplified our grant application
- We increased funding for grantee indirect expenses
- There is now open dialogue about diversity, equity and inclusion throughout the organization
- We recognize grantee changemakers at the Annual Report to the Community
- We hosted an impactful Summit on Race Matters series in 2020-21 after the George Floyd murder
- We have an updated employee handbook
- We now have a compensation philosophy and salary bands for every position

My KISRA experience informed the strategies I have deployed at TGKVF, for example the capacity building work to strengthen grantee partners. The authors of a 2020 article in Stanford Social Innovation Review define capacity building as, "the process of building and strengthening the systems, structures, cultures, skills, resources, and power that organizations need to serve their communities." I know what it is like to build and operate a nonprofit. I therefore am very aware of the kinds of support our nonprofit partners need to be successful.

I am proud of the awareness we built through convening the Summit on Race Matters in West Virginia. From August 2020 through January 2021 TGKVF hosted the 2020 Summit on Race Matters in West Virginia. The Summit was designed to discuss race in a comprehensive, collaborative and compassionate manner in order to build what Martin Luther King, Jr. termed a "beloved community" in West Virginia.

While all West Virginians are integral to moving the state forward, Black West Virginians face systemic barriers that impede their full participation in this important work. The Summit was convened to address these barriers in a meaningful, sustainable and transformative way, so that all West Virginians can participate in a West Virginia renaissance.

Throughout six separate sessions (each 2.5-hours long), 28 speakers with expertise in the field of social justice discussed eight topic areas in the following order:

1. Understanding Racism
2. Criminal Justice
3. Civic Engagement
4. Health
5. Education and Employment
6. Housing and Wealth

Desired outcomes aimed to: strengthen the skills of individuals working to build communities that serve everyone; serve as an incubator for increased collaborative leadership in building these communities; raise awareness of systemic inequalities; and develop an agenda of thoughtful and visionary policies and practices that empower Black West Virginians, and thus the state and nation.

The key underlying theme running throughout the reports, and the most commonly expressed message from speakers, is that racism is deeply imbedded in American institutions and the psyche of the nation's citizens. This is a problem we must not look away from, but collectively tackle head-on through education, political engagement, government and institutional reforms and difficult conversations that can affect change. In short, regardless of skin color, we all have a duty to address racial inequality and inequity when we encounter it.

Summit panelists widely agreed that the roots of racism in America began with slavery. "It's impossible to grapple with where we are as a nation if we don't understand how we got here," said Nikole Hannah-Jones, creator of The 1619 Project. "If you understand that we were a country that believed you could buy and sell human beings the same way you would sell a cow or a piece of land, then you understand that we've always been a country that did not value Black lives, and you can draw those direct lines."

Many of those lines intersect with the topics explored in this report. Our broken criminal justice system, voter suppression and health disparities experienced by people of color are just a few of the challenges that non-White communities have faced for generations. Striking examples of inequality highlighted during the Summit and within this report include:

- Black Americans make up 40% of the prison population

despite representing only 13% of the US population.[1]

- African Americans experience the worst health care, the worst health status and the worst health outcomes of any racial or ethnic group in the US, according to the *Journal of the National Medical Association*.[2]
- Non-White school districts receive $23 Billion *less* than White districts despite serving the same number of students, according to a 2019 report by the nonprofit EdBuild.[3]
- Black students experience the highest rates of poverty, according to **Congress's** *Conditions of Education 2020* **report**.[4]
- A typical median net worth of a White family is about ten times the median net worth of a typical Black family.[5]

And in West Virginia:

- African Americans, despite representing around 3% of the population, are in prison at 3.5 times the rate of White people.[6]
- Black children are placed in detention centers 1.8 times more often than their White counterparts.[7]
- Black households have 70% of the income of White households.[8]

---

[1] https://www.prisonpolicy.org/reports/pie2020.html

[2] https://www.ncbi.nlm.nih.gov/pmc/articles/PMC2593958/

[3] https://edbuild.org/content/23-billion - CA

[4] https://nces.ed.gov/programs/coe/

[5] https://www.cnn.com/2020/06/03/politics/black-white-us-financial-inequality/index.html

[6] Statistic provided by panelist Kitty Dooley

[7] Statistic provided by panelist Kitty Dooley

[8] https://wvpolicy.org/wp-content/uploads/2020/11/SWWV-2020-1109-Final.pdf

- Black men and Black women have higher unemployment rates. [9]
- Black West Virginians experience disparities in education, health, and earnings outcomes and within the criminal justice system.[10]

In 2020, the COVID-19 pandemic and murder of George Floyd by a Minneapolis police officer served to highlight long-standing racial inequalities in the US. While these recent events and the Black Lives Matter movement have sparked a conversation around the need for racial justice, the Summit made it clear that much work is left to be done. To accelerate these efforts, a host of recommendations for combating racism in the spheres of criminal justice, civic engagement, health, education, employment, housing and wealth are compiled in the summit report.

Key Recommendations

What policymakers and businesses can do:

- Implement a community-level approach to the Defund the Police movement, which means finding ways to keep communities safe without pouring 50% of budgets into policing. Redirect monies into services—such as mental health, homelessness or possible suicides—so that incident calls are no longer turned over to the police, often producing horrible outcomes.

---

[9] https://wvpolicy.org/wp-content/uploads/2020/11/SWWV-2020-1109-Final.pdf
[10] https://wvpolicy.org/wp-content/uploads/2020/11/SWWV-2020-1109-Final.pdf

- Practice restorative justice, which focuses on rehabilitation and reconciliation.
- Fund the court system with tax dollars and expunge the criminal records and criminal court debt for every person in the US who has committed a nonviolent drug-related offense. This would help lift entire Black, Brown and rural communities across the nation out of economic decay.
- Fund community organizations and projects that support civic engagement and not larger businesses or corporations.
- Look at issues around social inequities within your own corporation, business, school, government, or agency. Examine all policies and make sure they're not worsening racial disparities.
- If you're a physician, be engaged and talk about the broader framework of health. Physicians have a front row seat to all of the parameters that contribute to outcomes.
- Make the right thing to do the easy thing to do. Instead of a trip to the hospital, create opportunities to get health needs met at schools and elsewhere in the community. Give those entities, organizations and social service agencies the resources they need to meet people where they are.
- Implement system-wide policies and practices that prevent exploitation and misapplication of rules. Detention becomes a feeder system into jail. "We should have zero tolerance for zero tolerance," said Michael Eric Dyson.
- When developing housing policies, even if they're good, universal policies, understand it's going to look differently

to different people based on underlying structures. Focus on, target and addresses issues of the most marginalized groups to make policies and solutions the most effective.

What ordinary citizens can do:

- Lead by example.
- Encourage children to read and learn about history, and not just White history.
- Find and attend local meetings; build relationships.
- Get children engaged in the political process; take them to the capitol.
- Get involved with Show Up for Racial Justice (https://www.showingupforracialjustice.org/), an organization primarily formed by White people to begin the process of eliminating racism.

"In West Virginia that has to be emphasized," said Angela Davis. "It's not only a Black struggle with a few White allies. It's a struggle for democracy for everyone."

We hope the findings and recommendations from the Summit, many of which stem from what Black, Indigenous, and People of Color (BIPOC) communities have themselves asked for over many years, will serve as a call to action for citizens, policymakers and business and institutional leaders to actively embrace anti-racism in the places they live, work, and govern.

Having worked to raise awareness, the next step was to move from awareness into action. Thus, the 2021 Summit on Race

Matters in West Virginia was convened to focus on actions taken by community leaders within their companies and organizations to address diversity, equity and inclusion (DEI). These leaders were invited to the conversation not because they are experts on race issues but because their organizations are taking action on matters of race.

Two back-to-back panels, with seven speakers on each panel, gathered to discuss the ways in which their companies and organizations are addressing DEI – first by short presentations within their respective organizations, followed by a Q&A session. Questions were submitted by community members prior to the event and facilitated by attorneys Kitty Dooley and Tom Heywood.

"We are not here to pat ourselves on the back in any way. We are here to share what steps we've taken to become more diverse and inclusive and equitable in our organization," explains panelist Shayla Leftridge, Director of Community Outreach for DEI at WV Health Right. "And we're very much here to hold ourselves accountable, to encourage other organizations to hold themselves accountable, and for leaders to hold other leaders accountable."

Depending on the nature of each panelist's business, actions to address diversity, equity and inclusion differed. Many lessons learned thus far, however, were similar, and all panelists voiced an eagerness to listen and learn from each other. In fact, listening and learning, then incorporating what has been heard and learned into a strategy, was fundamental to a successful approach.

Panelists unanimously agreed that DEI must become embedded into the fabric of companies and organizations by deliberate and intentional actions. Uncomfortableness will exist; hard conversations will be had, but do not let it be a roadblock. Continue on the journey for equality, and understand that it's a marathon, not a sprint.

We hope the actions and recommendations taken by the leaders of these organizations will help promote ideas and inspiration for other business leaders and interested parties that are looking to advance DEI in their workplaces and communities.

Reports from both summit series are available on www.racematterswv.tv

Chapter 21
Living My Best Life

I am living my life like it's golden. Jill Scott

I enjoy a fulfilling life in Charleston, West Virginia. Faith, family and philanthropy are my top priorities.

I am a Christian. I believe in God. I believe God fearfully and wonderfully made me. I believe he has been the maestro, orchestrating my life. In him I live and breathe and have my being. I am not perfect, never been perfect, but he loves me as I am, even with my rough spots. Even when I am unlovable; he keeps on loving me.

My faith in God sustains me. When I am faced with a new challenge, I seek his guidance through prayer. I don't panic. I seek his guidance. I remind him about his promises. And I am always amazed when I see him move on my behalf. He just shows up and shows out!

I am still a member of Ferguson Memorial Baptist Church in West Dunbar, West Virginia. I am honored to be their Minister of Administration under the leadership of Pastor Emanuel Alphonso Heyliger. In this role, I perform highly responsible, advanced level administrative support to the Pastor and church ministries; provide leadership in the planning, implementing, directing and reviewing of church programs; prepare and manage the church operations budget; and serve in a liaison role with the Deaconate relative to church administration.

I am blessed with a loving and supportive family, and I make spending time with them a priority. They include my parents, Winston and Muline Mickle; my siblings, Winston Mickle, Jr. and Melissa Mickle-Hope; my nephews, Winston Mickle, III and Jordan Hope; and my niece Makaila Hope. My extended family includes numerous aunts, uncles and cousins in the US and Guyana.

I am forever grateful for my late aunt Dolly Chesney who sponsored us to come to the United States and my aunt Norma Amsterdam who accommodated us in our early days in the United States. My love for my family is unconditional.

Your career can become all-consuming, but always be available for your loved ones, your family, your extended circle of family and friends. Always stay in touch, show up for holidays, birthdays, recitals, graduations, weddings, cookouts, etc. Schedule the time off, just like you schedule your business commitments. People remember how you made them feel. When you show up, they will feel good and remember you fondly. You don't ever want to look back after a loved one has passed and wish that you were more present.

Philanthropy is not only my career but my lifestyle. I liberally give of my time, talents and treasures in numerous ways. Here are a few:

- Appalachia Funders Network (Co-chair)
- African American Philanthropy in Action Giving Circle (Founding Member)
- Charleston-Institute (WV) Chapter of The Links Incorporated (President)
- Charleston Institute Alumnae Chapter of Delta Sigma Theta Incorporated (WV Program Planning & Development Liaison)
- Charleston Regatta (Commissioner)
- Charleston Rotary (2022-23 President Elect)
- Invest Appalachia (Board Member)
- Philanthropy WV (Board Member)
- Women for Economic Leadership and Development (Board Member)
- WV Women's Business Center (Advisory Council Member)

Additionally, I feel blessed to have had the opportunity to give back to Guyana. Volunteer efforts over the years have included planning, executing and evaluating a student conference at my high school (Queen's College of Guyana) that reached 250 annually; conducting a comprehensive needs assessment of my high school; facilitating West Virginia State University's recruiting and scholarship efforts in Guyana; co-hosting a visual literacy project team which resulted in the publishing of a book; and donating school supplies to my elementary school.

Even though I have a busy life, I do make time for fun. I host Fostering Solutions, a podcast that uplifts people and enterprises making positive impact in communities around the world. Episodes can be found on all major podcast sites. I enjoy the symphony (have season tickets to the WV Symphony Orchestra) and theatrical productions, especially on Broadway. I love to soul-line dance, run, workout with a fitness trainer and play pickleball. I enjoy making scented candles for special events. I also love to travel.

As I look to the future, I still believe that my best is yet to come!

REFERENCES

Raviraj (2022). How to Write an Awesome Nonprofit Mission Statement.
https://donorbox.org/nonprofit-blog/
nonprofit-mission-statement
Retrieved 10/21/2022

Understand Sustainability. Washington University in St. Lewis.
https://www.sustaintool.org/psat/understand/ retrieved
11/7/2022

Bacon C, Malone S, Prewitt K, Hackett R, Hastings M, Dexter S and Luke DA. (2022). Assessing the sustainability capacity of evidence-based programs in community and health settings.

Whetten, D and Cameron, K (2011). Developing Management Skills.

Board Source (2016). Common Nonprofit Board Problems.
https://boardsource.org/resources/
common-nonprofit-board-problems/
retrieved 10/27/2022

US Census Bureau

Cilluffo, A and Cohn, D (2019). Demographic trends shaping the US and the world in 2019.
https://www.pewresearch.org/fact-tank/2019/04/11/6-
demographic-trends-shaping-the-u-s-and-the-world-in-2019/

Sixon-Fyle, Dolan, K, Hunt D and Prince, S (2020). Diversity Wins: How inclusion matters
https://www.mckinsey.com/featured-insights/
diversity-and-inclusion/diversity-wins-how-inclusion-matters

Johnston, R (2014). The Hope Quotient: Measure It. Raise It. You'll Never Be the Same.

Davis, S (2021). Diversity, Equity & Inclusion For Dummies

Morukian M. (2022). Diversity, Equity, and Inclusion for Trainers: Fostering DEI in the Workplace

Kelly M. Hannum, Jennifer Deal, Liz Livingston Howard, Linshuang Lu, Marian N. Ruderman, Sarah Stawiski, Nancie Zane, and Rick Price (2011). Emerging Leadership in Nonprofit Organizations: Myths, Meaning, and Motivations. (Greensboro, NC: Center for Creative Leadership).

Planning and Conducting Needs Assessments: A Practical Guide (1995)
NeighborWorks America (2006). Community Development Evaluation Storymap and Legend.

Shelton, S (2017). 10 keys to successful leadership https://www.linkedin.com/
pulse/10-keys-successful-leadership-sonya-shelton/

Bielaszka-DuVernay, C (2008). Leadership Ability—You Either Have It or You Don't, Harvard Business Review
https://hbr.org/2008/02/leadership-abilityyou-either-h

Winsborough, D and Chamorro-Premuzic, T (2017). Great Teams Are About Personalities, Not Just Skills. Harvard Business Review

Lasker, R and Weiss, E (2003). Creating Partnership Synergy: The Critical Role of Community Stakeholders

W.K. Kellogg Foundation (2004). Logic Model Development Guide. https://wkkf.issuelab.org/resource/logic-model-development-guide.html

Association of Fundraising Professionals Resources. https://afpglobal.org

Rivera, J (2014). Community Development Utilizing Logic Models

Hummel, J. (1996). Starting and running a nonprofit organization

2020 Summit on Race Matters in West Virginia Compendium (2021). The Greater Kanawha Valley Foundation.

Union Carbide Corporation. https://www.unioncarbide.com/

About Form 1023, Application for Recognition of Exemption Under Section 501(c)(3) of the Internal Revenue Code. https://www.irs.gov/forms-pubs/about-form-1023

Pioneer Clubs: Helping Children Follow Christ in Every Aspect of Life.
https://www.pioneerclubs.org/about-us/

The Center for Communities that Care.
https://www.communitiesthatcare.net/

Walter, E (2013). 5 Myths Of Leadership. Forbes Magazine.
https://www.forbes.com/sites/ekaterinawalter/2013/10/08/5-myths-of-leadership/?sh=365a1fe7314e

Cherry, K (2022). 10 Tips for Becoming a Better Leader.
https://www.verywellmind.com/
ways-to-become-a-better-leader-2795324

Made in the USA
Columbia, SC
20 April 2025

56855350R00117